The Sto:

A New Zealan

Jane Mander

≈

FOR MY FAMILY
WITH LOVE

Books are not absolutely dead things, but do contain a
potency of life in them to be as active as that soul whose
progeny they are; nay they do preserve as in a vial the purest
efficacy and extraction of that living intellect that bred them.
– John Milton, *Areopagitica*

THE STORY OF
A NEW ZEALAND WRITER
JANE MANDER

≈

Rae McGregor

University of Otago Press

≈

Published by University of Otago Press
PO Box 56/56 Union Street, Dunedin, New Zealand
Fax: 64 3 479 8385.
Email: university.press@stonebow.otago.ac.nz

First published 1998
ISBN 1 877133 37 X

Cover design by Suellen Allen
Author photo by Gavin McGregor
Map by John McMeeking
Typeset by Egan-Reid Ltd, Auckland
Printed by GP Print Ltd, Wellington

Contents

≈

ILLUSTRATIONS

Pages 16-32
The milling settlement of Mander and Bradley at Raekau.
An example of a bush farmhouse – the Forde home at Pukekaroro.
Felling a big kauri at Griffin Road, Maungaturoto.
Mander's Mill Dam on the Waiariki River, Puhipuhi, c. 1902.
The Mander Dam at Puhipuhi, after being tripped, c. 1902.
Kauri logs at Whakapara, c. 1902.

Pages 48-64
The Mander home at Hatea Drive, Whangarei, in 1906.
Jane Mander with Miss Marshall and Miss V. Hosking, at Hatea Drive c. 1908-09.
Tea and biscuits: Miss V. Hosking and Jane Mander, c. 1908-09.
Jane Mander (centre) with Miss V. Hosking (left) and Miss Marshall at the back
of the Mander home (yes??) in Hatea Drive, Whangarei. Whangarei Museum
A bush picnic, c. 1910.
Whangarei Tennis Club, c. 1910.
Whangarei Golf Club, c. 1910.
Jane Mander, dressed ready to leave home, on the steps of the house at Hatea
Drive, c. 1910. Whangarei Museum
Janet Mander, c. 1912.
The home of Susannah Clayton at Stewarts Bay, on the Kaiwaka River, 1971.

Pages 80-96
Jane Mander's passport photograph, 1914.
Columbia University, New York, 1995.
Barnard College, New York, 1995.
117 Waverly Place, New York.
Published author. Jane in New York in 1920.
Another portrait, sometime in the 1920s, possibly in New York.
Jane's home in London – 49 Cathcart Road, Chelsea.
Jane as a London flapper in the 1920s.
Two photographs of Jane published in the *Mirror*, 1 January 1932.
A portrait of Jane Mander as distinguished novelist.

PREFACE

≈

This is the first Christmas I won't be sending blue cornflowers to Jane Mander. She died on Tuesday at Whangarei. She loved blue. She had blue eyes, blue Chinese vases, and blue in her Persian rugs, and she always loved cornflowers.

It is hard to think of Jane's vitality laid to rest. She had the magnificent Mander energy that should have carried her into her 90s, as it did her father. Instead, it drove her until it wore her out in her 70s: yet still a young woman, little more than a girl, in her outlook.

I always thought of Jane as a contemporary instead of a person twice my age. She was eternally youthful. The years only deepened her maturity and widened her outlook.

It is one of the tragedies of New Zealand letters that Jane Mander wrote her books when she was young. She is, perhaps, the only typical New Zealand writer whose characters are unashamedly New Zealanders who move naturally against a New Zealand background, because it is their background, who are of the soil, the sea, the sky, typical of their country.

The Story of a New Zealand River is the best New Zealand book ever written. If it had been written by Jane 25 years later it would have been one of the great novels of its time.

As it was, it had Jane's freshness, her vitality, her tolerance, her love of beauty in every shape and form, but it might too, have had her great maturity, a quality few adults ever live long enough to acquire.

Jane spent some time during the first World War in the United States working with the Red Cross. She worked hard, acquiring the ghost of an American accent and an admiration for the American outlook, so like her own, keen, alert, unconditioned.

This time was also her most productive of writing.

Latterly, she read widely, did reviews for local periodicals and lived in and graced a room dominated by a picture of young Jane looking majestically down upon the world – a woman with coiled-up masses of red hair and cornflower blue eyes.

It is hard to think of such a woman dead.[1]

This graceful obituary by May Knight sums up the impact and influence Jane Mander had on many people who met her during her lifetime. It is also one of the best descriptions of her physical appearance.

In contrast, a rather gushy article by Freda Sternberg, which appeared in the March 1924 edition of *The Bookman*, describes Jane as tall 'with an abundance of corn-coloured hair and blue intelligent eyes'. And her passport, dated 1923, from the Consul General in New York, notes that her hair colour was blonde.

Most people who met Jane and mentioned any of her physical attributes, however, remembered the blueness of her eyes rather than the colour of her hair. Her eyes were keenly observing, they glinted with humour when she was amused, and sparked with anger when she thought someone was being treated unjustly.

May Knight says that Jane's most productive writing time was when she lived in New York. In some respects this was true, for it was there that she at last had a critical audience for her work, first at Barnard College, and then through the various intellectual groups with which she came in contact. She wrote two novels and numerous articles for periodicals in New York, before leaving to live in London. But she worked hard in London, too, and wrote four novels, as well as short stories for any paper which would take her work. She also wrote regular articles for New Zealand newspapers. On her return to New Zealand, Jane continued working hard as a reviewer, reading an enormous number of books and writing strong and pertinent reviews, which are still arresting to read sixty years later.

While it is debatable as to whether *The Story of a New Zealand River* is the best New Zealand book ever written, it did cut the tired connections of the Victorian novels which had formed the basis for New Zealand literature. And, despite the faults that Jane was to find in her book later, it did portray real New Zealanders who spoke in their own idiom. The cultural rawness of Tom Roland is set against the background of a pioneer country which is being stripped of its forests for profit and agriculture. And the author succeeded in creating characters which appeared unconventional at the time because she frankly discussed male and female relationships.

The Story of a New Zealand River can be looked upon as the literary bridge which opened the way for writers to depict their country in its true light. This fresh approach to writing about New Zealand has meant that in the latter part of the twentieth century Jane Mander is regarded as a pioneer figure in our literature.

RAE McGREGOR
Mangawhai, May 1998

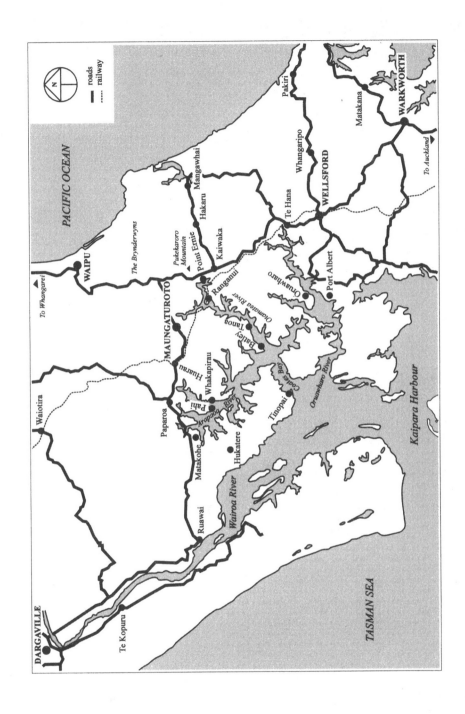

The North: the area in which Jane Mander spent her early years, and which features in most of her novels.

CHAPTER ONE

≈

I want to go away. I want to earn my own living. I want to see the world.
Asia in *The Story of a New Zealand River*

Miss Jane Mander elder daughter of Mr F. Mander M.P. for Marsden (who himself left the district to live in Auckland) today bade Whangarei what is to be a long adieu as she intends to take a four year study course at Columbia University U.S.A. Miss Mander will spend a couple of months in England before sailing to New York.

These few lines in the social column appeared in the *Northern Advocate* of March 1912. Their brevity gives no indication of the difficulties which Jane had overcome in order to leave for London and New York, hoping to fulfil her ambition of becoming a published novelist.

In literary matters the early 1900s were a desert in New Zealand. Financially or philosophically, there was no support for writers; like many other New Zealand artists, Jane Mander left the country in order to concentrate on her work. Further, she needed to get away from the fetters of family, to explore new ideas and to become part of a wider, more intellectual world.

In the small community art tends to be conservative, traditional conformist... Distance lends perspective though not enchantment to the exile. Distance gives perspective and for exiles it is also the prerequisite for freedom in their art. Freedom to write is a major stimulus to exile and exile creates the kind of isolation which is the nearest thing to freedom that a twentieth century artist is like to attain.[1]

The journey in 1912 was not the first time Jane had left the constricting shores of New Zealand. In 1907 she had visited Sydney for a few months. Then in 1910 she returned and stayed for almost a year. This time, however, her overseas journey would be much longer. Convincing her parents that she should leave home and make a life elsewhere – that she should have a career other than marriage – was not an easy thing to do. Her mother was semi-invalid, her father was relying on Jane to assist him with his parliamentary plans. She was thirty-five years old, and if she didn't marry, she should at least devote herself to the care and comfort of her parents.

It seemed quite unreasonable to her parents that their daughter, now approaching middle-age, should want to go to another part of the world to attend University. As well, even though she had matriculated, she had no secondary school education: how would she manage the study at university level? Jane prevailed, and not only did she finally have her parent's grudging approval, but her father agreed to give her a small allowance to help with her expenses.

In a letter to her sister Amy (always known in the family as Tommy) Jane gives some advice, telling her to take life as easily as she can and not to 'worry about any damned thing. When I think of how much better I am since I ceased to bother about what happened to me! it's amazing. As a family we've nearly all driven ourselves mad through it. I'd like to know at any time what remarks father makes about me in my absence. It won't hurt me, and might be useful.'[2] It is tantalising to speculate on what did happen between Jane and her parents but what is evident is that it had been a struggle for her to break away from home. She later commented that she had been marvellously well since leaving home, which is another indication of the stress she had suffered in making the break.

Jane was not the only New Zealand writer who struggled to shake off the shackles of her parents, although she may have been one of the earliest. Sixteen years later, Ngaio Marsh felt the burning heat of need to get away from her family, in particular her dominant mother, in order to explore her own artistic resonance. And like Jane, Ngaio was a woman in her mid thirties who had the confusion of feeling an 'an inward rage of compassion and resentment' when her mother could not accept that it was time for Ngaio to free herself from her mother's dominance and 'make her own choices in life'.[3]

The *Corinthic*, a three-class passenger ship, was berthed in Wellington. Jane was listed as a saloon passenger having paid £80 for the voyage which would take her to London via Monte Video, Rio de Janeiro and Tenerife. On 16 May 1912 her tall lithe figure walked up the gangway of the *Corinthic* and, as the ship sailed out past Pencarrow Head, her great adventure began. In her luggage was the manuscript of a novel which she hoped would be published when she got to London.

Jane Mander's family thought that she would be away for four years to study in New York. Perhaps Jane thought that too. She was to stay away from New Zealand for twenty years.

The novel which Jane took with her on the ship was not *The Story of a New Zealand River*, as many people have thought. She sets the record straight in a brief biography to Johannes Andersen in 1935: 'I took with me a first novel, not the Story of a New Zealand River, as has been erroneously stated. This book was turned down with admirable promptitude by four publishers. Among them was the late Mr Heinemann, who saw me personally and gave me half an hour of the best criticism and advice I have had from anybody. It was a sad pity that I did not afterwards send the New Zealand River to him.'

Despite her novel being turned down, Jane had a wonderful time when she arrived in London. The six weeks that it took for the ship to get to England via Cape Horn meant there was time for friendships to develop. Jane shared a cabin with Cushla Dumergue and they became good friends. By the time they finally reached London, Jane and Cushla had agreed to look for somewhere to stay together. They found a small hotel which suited them both. Cushla was younger and according to Jane very pretty, so the young men they had met on the boat soon arrived to escort her around London. Jane was also included in the invitations, for although she was older she was always popular with younger people.

In a letter to her sister Tommy, she talks about the cost of things in London, and her concern at managing on the allowance supplied by her father. But most obvious in the letter is the great enjoyment she had from finally being in London, of being able to visit art galleries and to have freedom of movement without the censure of a small community:

> *I'm going to have a tussle to get through on the money he's sending me. It seems it will only pay for 9 months at the University. I had forgotten all about the three months' vacation. I've saved what I could out of my London money, but have had to pay £15 for passage to America. I've schemed at sales and bought clothes at a marvellously cheap rate to last me for two years. I've thought often of you and wished I could get things out to you. You should see the dear little hat that cost me 2/7/1/2d trimmed by myself. It's quite ridiculous how you can get things at the sales. So I made hay while the sun shone for clothes are awfully expensive in New York, and it actually pays Americans to take the trip over [to England] to buy clothes. Thanks to men off the boat I've had a swimming time without having to pay for it. Board, of course, is dear here. I've paid 30/- a week for a top back room without extras. I've indulged in some luxuries, of course. I've had my hair most beautifully done. It looks just like it did when I was a girl, and will last a year. Cost me 30/- and was worth it. The man taught me how to do it myself. I am really fatter at last.*
>
> *I've seen a wonderful lot of London in the time. The picture galleries are just a delight, and the music halls are great. But if one never saw anything but the streets, the parks, the bridges, and the Thames it would be worth coming to see.*

This is a comfortable place. The servants are charming and have been dears to me. Four days ago two young Australian fellows about 30, awfully jolly, came here, and Miss Dumergue (girl off boat who is here with me) and I liked them at once, so they were put at our table and we chummed up with a rapidity that scandalised some of the sweet correct English ladies here. Indeed we laughed ourselves into hysterics on the stairs, and finally went out after tea to walk over one of the London bridges, this the very first day we'd spoken to them. They're great fun and know Sydney and Melbourne politicians. Miss D is very pretty and plays very well, and one of the boys plays the violin, so last night we had a concert here, and won the hearts of the old ladies, who love music. We're so glad the boys have come. They are so funny and friendly, and quite reliable, and we had no permanent men before.

Next week I'll post Riro [Jane's niece] an illustrated book of the Zoo (a wonderful place). I've lent it at present, and hope it won't be lost, as the children would love to see the very animals I've seen. ... Mr Holmes, man off boat, who is fond of Cushie (Miss D.) has been taking us out a bit to dinner and music halls. You get lovely music and little plays at the halls and you can smoke, and have tea and drinks – just like a free and easy entertainment, and the buildings are gorgeous and the seats lovely. He always takes us to the orchestra stalls. I suppose I've seen easily over 30 entertainments of one sort and another since coming here. But all the same I'm dying to get to the university and settle down to work. I know I shall love Americans. Some have stayed here and they are just charming. They are the most friendly people under Heaven.

I've been marvellously well since leaving home. Never have a pang, and hope I'll keep so....

I leave for America a week on Friday, by a big slow liner – takes seven days. You know my University address – Whittier Hall, Columbia University, New York City. Shall be so delighted to have the photos of the children – love to them all and Jim.

Best love

Jane

Give my love to all Whangarei friends[4]

Chapter Two

≈

The first thing that struck Alice about it all
was its appalling isolation.
The Story of a New Zealand River

Jane's journey to England in 1912 was, in some ways, reversing the voyage which both sets of grandparents had made over fifty years before. Her paternal grandparents, John and Jane Mander, emigrated to New Zealand on the *Ramillies* in 1847. John Mander was a private in the Royal Marines and was part of the first Fencible detachment to arrive in Auckland. The name Fencible came from the word 'defensible', used in the sixteenth century in Britain to describe men who were fit enough for military service. The New Zealand Fencibles were men who were on pensions from the British Army.

Governor Grey had requested a militia for his colony, to protect the European settlements from Maori insurgents. The British Army had too many men on pensions, and so it seemed a simple answer to allow the pensioners to go to New Zealand to form a home guard.

The men were enrolled in Britain and sent with a one-way ticket. They were expected to act as colonists and take up civilian occupations, but should the need for troops arise the Fencibles would move into the positions usually taken by regular troops in a garrison and defend the town from any attack. The Fencibles enlisted for a term of seven years, and were promised a free passage to New Zealand for themselves and their wives; they were also promised a cottage and an acre of land. If they wanted more land, they were expected to purchase it for themselves, as no further grants were to be made to them. Over 2500 men, women and children arrived in Auckland under this scheme, which was the only organised form of colonisation experienced there.

So that the families who were coming to New Zealand in the Fencible contingent could set up house, the men were allowed to take an advance on their pensions to buy such necessities as clothing and household linen. Once in New Zealand, tools to work their acre of land could be bought from the government stores. They were expected to find work in Auckland, and as there was a shortage of labour it was supposed that this would happen. If they could not find work in the first year they would be guaranteed government work.

The amount of the pension varied, being sixpence to ninepence a day for privates, and NCOs and Officers received more. John Mander's pension was about 1/6 per day so he may well have been an NCO, although according to the Fencible records he was a private.

John Mander was the youngest of nine children and was born in North Piddle, Worcestershire. His family were farmers, but following the Napoleonic wars there was a severe agrarian depression and little work for boys on farms. It is not known for sure, but it is believed that John Mander was making his way home from Plymouth when he was caught by a Royal Marine recruiting party at Frome, Somerset. His attestation is dated 13 January 1821. In 1841 he married Jane Amphlett who was born in 1814 at Great Hampton, near Evesham, Worcestershire, just down the road from North Piddle. They had four children born in England: Edmund William (1842), Mary Jane (1843), Amelia (1845), and John Jordan Jnr (1847). Young John was just eight weeks old when the family boarded the *Ramillies* for New Zealand.[1] John Mander was forty-five when he arrived in New Zealand, and he was described as being 5ft 8in tall, with dark hair going bald, blue eyes, a fresh complexion and a very good industrious character. His occupation was recorded as farm labourer. He was discharged at his own request, and it is noted that his left leg was broken, so it may have been thought that he was not fit to stay as part of the Fencible contingent. Of his wife Jane, there is no description.

The Manders settled first at Alfred Street in Onehunga with other members of their company, but later they lived at Otahuhu, and at Papakura. In 1848 Francis Mander was born at Onehunga, and in 1852 the Mander family moved to a farm at Papakura, where their last child Sarah Ann was born on 14 September 1853.

The Manders did not prosper, which was often the fate of Fencible families; many were illiterate, and work was often spasmodic. Despite their lack of prosperity John Mander lived until he was eighty-seven, still collecting his 1/6 per day, and died in October of 1889. Nothing is noted of his wife.

By the time Francis Mander was ten he was out earning a living. Frank worked as a farm labourer and also went prospecting for gold in the Coromandel. Hard work and entrepreneurial skills meant that by the time Frank was twenty-eight he owned 100 acres of land in South Auckland.

Jane's maternal grandparents arrived in New Zealand from Yorkshire in October 1859 on the *Shalimar*. They had paid a fare of £87/10/- for the

≈ Top: The milling settlement of Mander and Bradley at Raekau. On the hill is the Mander house and to the right are logs awaiting trimming and milling. Matakohe Kauri Museum

≈ Bottom: An example of a bush farmhouse – the Forde home at Pukekaroro, built in 1863. Matakohe Kauri Museum

≈ FELLING A BIG KAURI AT GRIFFIN ROAD, MAUNGATUROTO. MATAKOHE
KAURI MUSEUM

journey. William Kerr was thirty-three years old and his wife Ann Mary was thirty when they arrived, and they had four children with them. Janet Kerr, who was to be Jane Mander's mother, was one of those children, she was just two years old. The Kerrs brought with them the accoutrements of what was considered necessary for a civilised life: books, paintings, and silverware inscribed with the Kerr initials, and a staunch belief in the Protestant religion.

After arriving in New Zealand, the Kerrs lived first in Auckland for two years and then bought a property at Ramarama on the Great South Road. The land was good, and it was accessible by the only metalled road in the province, the military highway through to the Waikato River.[2] However, they were there for only two years when war erupted and raids from the Maori flowed onto the Kerr land. The Kerrs buried treasures in the orchard and hurriedly left. A very large Victorian lithograph called 'The Last Judgement', which the Kerrs had brought with them from England, was left hanging on the wall. It was far too bulky for the family to hide or to carry with them. When it was safe for the family to return to their home, the house had been ransacked, everything that was portable had been taken, all that is, except the lithograph. Across the wooden floor were footprints leading to the picture, the footprints stopped in front of the picture, and then the footprints retreated. It had obviously been perused and the Maori had made the same decision as the Kerrs: that it was best left where it was.

Eventually the picture came into Jane Mander's possession, and in her will she left it to her sister Annie. On Annie's death it was bequeathed to the Auckland Institute and Museum. It is now catalogued and is regarded as an interesting example of a Victorian engraving by John Martin. Not everyone would regard it as an image to look at daily. It has a strong Protestant message. The Avenging Angel holding a lightning bolt hovers in the centre of the picture above the pit of Hell, into which slide all those who are not saved. Those sliding into the black gaping abyss include clergy in jewelled clothes, soldiers and all aspects of fighting, elephants and horses, and a train with open carriages which has Moscow, London, Paris, written on individual carriages. Those who are saved (who sit high in the light on the left-hand side of the picture) are mothers and babies, and clergy without jewels (obviously Protestant). It is no wonder the Maori left it hanging on the wall. Warwick Lawrence remembers seeing the lithograph hanging in Jane's house in Remuera in the 1930s; when he saw it a look of horror must have come over his face because Jane laughed and said, 'The Pater's taste in art'.[3]

The Kerrs were not wealthy but they placed value on reading, music and art, and they had an inbuilt regard for education. Walter Kerr, Janet Kerr's youngest brother, and Jane Mander's uncle, was to become a scholar. With little early formal education he went on to gain an Arts degree from the New Zealand University, and was one of the first graduates from Auckland University College. This intellectual ability, and the determination to attain an education against all odds, was repeated when Jane succeeded with her matriculation in New Zealand (after studying for it at night), and later with top marks at Barnard College. Her love for reading, music and art were as much a part of her inheritance as was the painting of 'The Last Judgement'.

Francis Mander, the hard-working extrovert, courted the quiet shy Janet Kerr and they were finally married on 18 May 1876. at Janet's home 'Springfield' at Ramarama. Janet's parents, sister, brothers, and cousins were all witnesses at the marriage, but oddly no Mander names appear on the record as witnesses. The newly married couple set up their home on the land which Frank had bought in 1875. It was nearly a year after their marriage on 9 April 1877 that their first child was born. She was named Mary Jane after her aunt and her two grandmothers. Four more children followed: Francis Herbert in 1878, Carrie Emily in 1880, Anne Gertrude in 1884, and Amy Violet (known as Tommy) in 1886.

With a new baby and a 100 acres of land, it appeared that the Frank Manders were destined to be settlers in Ramarama, their life repeating that of other young couples making their way in a still raw country. However, Frank Mander the entrepreneur was never going to be happy with staying put on a small holding. He had dreams of greater things, and it was to the great kauri trees that he turned his attention. For his young wife it would mean learning to make a home almost anywhere that there was kauri to mill. Jane said that, 'We moved as many as twenty-nine times in a few years. Often as many as three times a year'.[4] City-dwellers would find it difficult even to imagine what moving meant in those days when travelling was possible only in the most crude conveyance. Men, women children, animals and furniture were all bundled in together. Often the family home would be a deserted store, or a mud whare. Domestic arrangements were ignored by Frank. Janet Mander had to make the best of each situation, trying to create a home in often impossible places. Such practicalities as getting clothes clean were of little importance, when there was a chance of finding timber to cut. On one occasion Janet Mander had just put the weekly wash to soak in old kerosene tins when Frank came home and said they would be moving the next day.

In their desire to have a garden of their own, the women of the Mander family would uproot the flowers from one garden – roses, geraniums, mignonette and sweet peas – and take them on the journey in the vain hope that they would flower afresh in a new setting.[5]

Moving so often meant that the family lived in and upon boxes. Such things as ornaments, necessary in any Victorian household, suffered sadly. As Jane said 'in those days a broken treasure was a calamity. As a reward for specially good behaviour my mother would open a tin-lined case in which she kept some of the few things that had been overlooked by the Maori when they wrecked my grandfather's house during the war. Anyone can visualise the contents of that box of Georgian and early Victorian bric-a-brac, needlework, old silver and china and jewellery. There has never been in my life a box more full of enchantment. Even the tissue paper wrappings were fragrant with the English associations that tug so at the heart of exiles.'[6]

In *The Story of a New Zealand River*, Jane describes the house that Alice comes to after her first trip down the river. It was the type of house the Mander family would have often lived in, a house close to where the timber was being milled:

> The front door opened straight into the 'sitting room', which led directly into the front bedroom. The kitchen and Asia's room at the back had yet to be boarded in and lined. Then there was to be a lean-to to contain a scullery and a small porch.
>
> The house stood well off the ground on wooden blocks through which the wind could blow what tune it pleased. There was no question of painting it or finishing it in any way. Of course the boss had visions of something more later on. But this would have to do, perhaps for years. It was to be a makeshift, something in the nature of a picnic. Tom Roland, who had lived most of his life in the open air, had acquired the picnic spirit. It had never occurred to him that it had to be acquired. He expected his wife to produce it immediately.[7]

Frank Mander had the same expectations of his wife Janet – it was left to her to run the household, to see that the children were educated, while he, Frank, explored the country for kauri to mill.

In New Zealand the kauri tree was the wealth of the North, as gold was the source of wealth for the South. The Maori had known the value of the kauri for a long time. Their canoes were made from it:.

> Major R.A. Cruise of H.M.S. *Dromedary* saw and measured a canoe hollowed from a solid trunk ... 84 feet in length 6 feet in width and 5 feet in depth. It was steered by a chief at the stern, and driven through the water with astonishing speed by 90 stalwart warriors equipped with paddles. Cruise says

that he saw canoes cross the Bay in seas so rough that it was considered imprudent to lower the ship's boats.[8]

Captain Cook must have also been aware of the kauri when he was in the Bay of Islands in 1769, but it was the French explorer Marion du Fresne who in 1772 brought the beautiful giant to the notice of Europe. On 3 April the ships *Mascarin* and the *Marquis de Castries* rounded Cape Maria van Diemen. After several weeks of bad weather, the *Marquis* had a damaged foremast and bowsprit. The ship put into the Bay of Islands for shelter and for repairs. Here they met with Maori who appeared friendly and who showed them a kauri forest near Manawaru Bay. A tree was selected and a spar sixty-five feet in length was cut and trimmed. M. Crozet, du Fresne's second in command, gave this description:

> The tree which prevails most of all in the forests is the olive-leafed cedar. I had cedars of this variety cut down whose trunks were more than a 100 feet long, from the ground to the lowest branches, and 52 inches in diameter. The trees are very resinous, the resin is white and transparent, and gives out an agreeable smell like incense when burnt ... its wood is elastic, and I judged it very suitable for making ships' masts.[9]

Unfortunately, du Fresne's kauri gatherers were killed by Maori before the foremast could be dragged to the shore. There may have been some violation of the forest, or maybe the members of the ship's company had fished in waters which were forbidden by Maori.

The value of the kauri soon became known in Europe. In 1783 James M. Matra described kauri planks as 'superior to any that Europe possesses', and he suggested that the British Government should fill returning ships with cargoes of kauri 'for use of the Kings yards'.[10]

It was not until 1820 that the first load of spars was shipped out on the *Dromedary*. There were ninety-eight spars cut from a stand of trees at Whangaroa. At that time it was estimated that north of a line drawn from Kawhia on the west coast and Katikati on the east, kauri forests covered an area of 3 million acres.[11] With that first shipment of timber for commercial purposes, the logging of the great forests had begun.

Frank Mander could see the market potential of kauri. In a young country people needed houses. What better product than a tree which grew straight and true, a timber known for its durability, and a tree which was accessible.

In *The Story of a New Zealand River* Jane models Tom Roland, the enterprising boss of the milling company, on her father. Tom Roland, using Frank Mander's opinions, explains the need to cut the kauri:

'There!' Roland put down the luncheon baskets he was carrying, and waved his hand airily at them. 'Best bit of bush in the colony. Nothing to beat it outside of California. Those trees have stood there thousands of years. Might have stood there thousands more.'

'And you are going to cut them down!' exclaimed Alice, as if it were sacrilege.

'You bet I am. Great job too. Takes some tackling.' He was proud that he had dared to stake everything he possessed on this great adventure. He knew that he was being discussed in Auckland business circles as a bold spirit and as a coming man.

'I've told you what I think about it,' said Mrs Brayton.

'Rot!' laughed Tom Roland. 'What would you have people live in in this country? Timber is cheaper than bricks. Those trees make houses for the poor. Somebody has to cut 'em down. Look at the people who can own their own houses in New Zealand. Why? Cheap land, cheap timber. Something you don't have in England.'[12]

Frank Mander always believed what he was doing was important. To house the people was paramount, the trees were there for the milling, the depredation of the forest was secondary to the need for housing.

Jane Mander used two of her main characters in *The Story of a New Zealand River*, Alice and Mrs Brayton, to point out that not everyone condoned the slaughter of the giant trees. The following description of the felling of a kauri tree underlines Jane's own feeling that it was close to vandalism when the giant trees were cut and reduced to a commercial commodity:

> The whole world seemed to lurch, slowly, slowly: then the top branches shook, the great trunk swayed, the foundations cracked. The whole tree gave one gigantic shiver, poised for an instant, suspended, hesitating, and then, realising as it were, the remorselessness of fate, it plunged forward, filling the whole visible world, and cracking horribly, till its longest branches caught the ground with a series of tearing, ripping sounds, preliminary to the resounding roar as the massive trunk struck and rebounded and rolled upon the earth. ...
>
> 'There, that's over,' said the boss cheerfully. 'I guess we can have lunch now. You stay here. This is a good place by the creek.'
>
> He could not understand why Alice had tears in her eyes, or why she looked at him as if he had committed a crime. He set off for the luncheon baskets, swinging his arms and whistling gaily. [13]

Later, when Jane was in London, she wrote an article comparing her life in London with that in New Zealand. It was evident that Frank Mander's views about milling the kauri were not shared by his daughter:

We had our skyscrapers in those days, but they were trees, trees that walled off the rest of the world and held up the sky. They were also our antiques, I thought them as old as God. My first sense of terror, of rage at the ruin of beauty came from seeing them cut down.[14]

The other wealth of the North of which Jane would write was the gumfields. Once again, Captain Cook had noticed the kauri gum: 'In speaking of Mercury Bay I had forgot to mention that the Mangrove trees there produce a resinous substance very much like resin...We found it, at first in small lumps on the sea beach'.[15]

Initially gum could be collected from the surface, residue jewels of the great prehistoric forests. Later when the gum was found to be useful for manufacturing varnish and later linoleum, the search for the gum intensified, and it had to be dug out of the ground. The gumdiggers became as much a part of the North as the kauri tree and its golden resin. In *The Story of a New Zealand River* and in *Allen Adair* Jane writes about the gumfields as she remembered them:

> It was true that the sprawling, undulating waste that stretched from his feet to hazy horizons was as bare and as bleak as he had expected it to be. There was no sign of man nor beast upon it. The season had passed it by. Alone of lands upon the river it wore no flush of green. Nothing had budded upon its niggardly soil. The stunted manuka was brown, the crawling lycopodium was brown, the very fern had a rusted look. Nowhere was there a sign of a complete and sizeable tree. And this where once there had flourished the most prolific of forests, and the most opulent of trees. Never had a prodigal nature left behind so little visible reminder of former wealth. The earth had borne too well and was shrivelled now in permanent exhaustion.

> But the old lure of hidden treasure was there under that barrenness.[16]

For the first time in literature, the North which had been overlooked and dismissed as not worthy of being the basis for any story was being brought to the light. Although later writers would disagree with Jane's description of the gumfield, she was the first writer who saw something beautiful and even mystical in the gumfields of the North.

From her ancestors Jane had inherited an energy and single-mindedness when approaching a goal. The pioneering antecedents were only two generations removed from her, and their tenacity at overcoming difficulties and making a life for themselves in a new country was something that Jane acquired along with her intellectual ability. From her gentle mother she inherited a sensitivity, and a tenderness which, while not always apparent on first meeting, benefited those who were to become her close friends.

Chapter Three

≈

*We need knowledge and we cannot begin too
soon to give knowledge to our children.*
David Bruce in *The Story of a New Zealand River*

In 1881 Frank Mander had been cutting timber at Awhitu at the
southern end of the Manukau Harbour, but it was not long before he
moved north to Wellsford. In 1883, Mary Jane Mander started school at
Wellsford Primary. She was probably dressed in the typical style of the
times – a dark dress with a starched white apron over it and button boots.
Jenny Mander, as she was entered in the school roll, was six years old
when she and her brother Bert went to school. Jane was a bright young
child and it is probable that she had been taught at home by her mother
until the family was settled in an area with a school close enough for the
children to walk.

The little Wellsford school had been the dream of the people of the
area, who were the pioneers of Port Albert. Settled by members of a non-
conformist church, Port Albert was sponsored by the Albertland Special
Settlement Association, set up in Birmingham in 1861 by William Rawson
Brame. It was named Albertland after Queen Victoria's husband. The
Association encouraged people from all walks of life to become part of a
great colonisation scheme. The idea was that Albertland would become a
city the size of Auckland, that it would allow freedom of worship and
maintain tolerance towards all religious persuasions.

With the object of community co-operation in view, provision was made
to have a portion of the settlement lands set apart and surveyed into small
sections for a township, the intention being that while the emigrants
should enter into colonial farming, the township should be the convenient
centre for business facilities, the establishment of the various artisans and
tradesmen who should serve the community, and the convenient centre
for church, school, public library, newspaper office, etc. In the vision of
this Albertland colony across the sea, the cultivation of the soil, the
provision for education and the nurture of religious life were wisely
planned.[1]

With their Protestant beliefs, the Manders would have fitted well into this pioneering community. At last Jane's mother Janet would have had a place which was congenial for her; the roughness of life in milling areas would be ameliorated in a strongly religious but tolerant society.

The name Wellsford is derived from the initial letters of the surnames of many of the early pioneers. Originally the name of the area was Whakapirau, but the early settlers didn't like the name, and confusion arose because of another 'Whakapirau' opposite Pahi. So they hit upon the original idea of renaming the area.[2] It was Mrs Rushbrook (one of the names listed in the 'R' of Wellsford) who set up the first school. She began a School for Young Ladies in a room of her home, a home which also doubled as the Post Office.

The settlers held a meeting, elected a school board and applied to the Education Board to build a school at Wellsford on the Education Reserve (Lot 129).[3] There must have been an element of frustration in the communication with the Education Board because eventually the Wellsford people built the school themselves and opened it on 1 April 1875. Mrs Rushbrook was appointed as School Mistress for a salary of £50 per annum. She was to be Jane's first teacher.

The school was typical of schools throughout New Zealand at the time. It was a single room with a gable porch at one end for the children to hang their coats and bags. In 1876 Mrs Rushbrook was complaining that the room was not fit in winter. Neither wind- nor water-tight, the room had no chimney. She was willing to take the children to her home for the winter months. She referred to the school as 'A miserable barn of a place, still without school furniture.'[4] It wasn't until 1877 that the desks and the teacher's table were completed. By the time Jane arrived at the school, there were desks for the children to sit at and the chimney and mantelpiece had been fixed. The school had been lined and so for the winter months the room would have been cosy.

Mrs Rushbrook had Jane in her class for a little over a year before the Manders moved on again and Jane was enrolled at Port Albert School on the Kaipara. Like the Wellsford school, this school had been erected by Albertland settlers. In 1874 a report on the school by an Education Board inspector stated, 'Roll 17 boys, 12 Girls. Maps sufficient, easel required. School conducted in fairly efficient manner'.[5] However, by the time Jane arrived at the school (which was run by Mr Benjamin Martin Gubb, always known as Benny Martin) it was properly equipped to teach children from primer classes upwards.

The roll was now in the vicinity of fifty pupils, and the teaching staff comprised Benny Martin, Miss Jane Cameron a pupil-teacher, and Miss Susan Becroft, who was the teacher employed to teach the girls sewing. It is difficult to imagine Jane settling down to instruction on sewing seams, as she later said that all domestic occupations bored her, but she obviously learnt enough to trim a hat. However, Jane's stay at Port Albert School was short. Frank Mander moved up to Pukekaroro to start logging timber in the forest there, and some of the Mander children went to Kaiwaka school. There is no record, though, of Jane being at that school, and so one of the many gaps in her formal education occurs. Whether she was sent away to school in Auckland or whether she was taught again at home by her mother is speculation. The physical difficulty of attending school in those days of clay tracks for roads was daunting. In the winter, after seemingly continuous rain, the clay tracks which were the dusty roads of summer became a thick claggy mire. Horses would be up to their withers in mud, so the chance of a small child managing to make her way to school on a wet and cold morning would be out of the question. Benny Martin's diary of 1882 at the Port Albert School notes 'March 14th Tues very wet and stormy – no school. March 15th Wed. Wet. Twelve at school ... June 9th Friday A poor school week.'[6]

When Jane was nine the family moved to live at Point Ernie, at the head of the Kaiwaka River. The house they came to was a change from some of the places they had called 'home'. This house was large and had been built the previous year. It was situated at Stewarts Bay, a local name for the bay, named after the people who owned the land surrounding the area. And it was here that the Manders would stay long enough for Jane to make some friends. Edith Hall, whose father was the tallyman for the Kauri Timber Company, and who also worked as Frank Mander's secretary, was the same age as Jane. She and Jane were friendly with the Coates girls: Mary, Beach and Minnie. The families would often join together for picnics in the bush, and it was these picnics and bush visits which were to imprint themselves on Jane's mind, to resurface when she wrote *The Story of a New Zealand River*.

It was also at Stewarts Bay that Jane met another person who was to have a strong influence on her, so strong an influence in fact that she was included in *The Story of a New Zealand River* as the kind and helpful Mrs Brayton. Mrs Susannah Clayton was a neighbour of the Manders. She lived in a two-storied house on a hill which overlooked the Kaiwaka River. Mrs Clayton was described as a woman who was energetic, who loved her garden, kept bees, and was an expert at making sauces and wines and preserves. She was not prepared to compromise her life, which was based on her previously comfortable London circumstances, to any wildness of the colonial situation. She had bought a small house and enlarged it for the comfort of herself and her son, and she included such luxuries as a bell pull device in the drawing room and the living rooms in order to summon the servants. That she had servants was an amazing anomaly in the remote areas of the north.

It was to this house that Jane would climb the hill, and it was from Mrs Clayton that she learnt there was more beyond the isolation of the kauri forest. It is probably here, too, that Jane's love of music was fostered. Mrs Clayton (like Mrs Brayton in *The Story of a New Zealand River*) owned a piano. She also had an extensive library, books which Jane could borrow; until this time the only book with coloured illustrations she had seen was the family bible. At a time when her formal education was disrupted, Mrs Clayton filled a gap. This was to benefit Jane for the rest of her life. Jane's gratitude towards Mrs Clayton is evident in her creation of the sympathetic character of Mrs Brayton in *The Story of a New Zealand River*, a character so loving and wise that when she dies in the novel something strong in the narrative goes.

By the time Jane was eleven the family had moved again, this time back to Port Albert. Her father, with his partner Mr S. Bradley, had built a sawmill at Raekau across the Oruawharo inlet from Port Albert. Frank Mander was held in high esteem in the area and it is said that the partnership of Mander and Bradley was sealed with a handshake. It was also said of Frank Mander that he was known for his sincere sympathy for his fellow humans, and that in periods of economic depression no swagman was turned away without a few days work and keep at Mander and Bradleys.[7] In 1887 Frank Mander applied to the Hobson County Council for permission to build roads and tramways into the bush to bring out the timber. This enormous undertaking, built by the hard physical labour of men, re-emerges in Jane's description of a tramway in her novel *The Passionate Puritan*. She describes the sensation, through her heroine Sidney Carey, of riding on a car on the tramway:

> After the horses were hitched to the trucks in tandem fashion they began slowly to ascend a long slope of even steepness. Almost immediately they plunged into high bush, the trees often meeting overhead. Sidney began to be thrilled. Down one side she saw a good way down into the depths of a ravine and heard water roaring out of sight at the bottom. On the other side she stared into tropical undergrowth that looked as if no man had ever worked his way through it. She knew it must have been a tough job to lay that railway there. She learned afterwards that Jack Ridgefield had engineered it and overseen its construction as a boy of twenty.[8]

Once again Jane attended Port Albert school as a pupil, but this time it was to be for a short time, as the family moved to Mangere. In March 1889 she started with her brother and sisters at the Onehunga School;

she was twelve. The Mander children walked about three miles to and from Onehunga School, crossing the Mangere Bridge. Getting to school in the relatively urban area of Onehunga would have been easy, in contrast to the dust and mud of the roads to the schools they had attended in the north. Jane, who had grown tall and with her fair pigtails flying, would stride the three miles with no difficulty at all.

School now meant that Jane could write compositions, and read as much as she liked. While the other girls at the school library would borrow books such as *What Katy Did* to read, Jane would be reading novels by Sir Walter Scott and Dickens. Her two school friends, Fanny and Ethel Tapp, were always amazed at the amount of reading she did, and that it was always books 'miles above our heads'.[9] From her days with Mrs Clayton, Jane had been encouraged to read books which would extend her intellect.

Her gift for story-telling was remembered by J.J.M. Mitchell, who recalls that she once told him that Te Kooti was 'out' – otherwise on the warpath. 'She described with gruesome detail, the infinite delight Te Kooti took in catching small boys playing on the road after dark – who would not go in when called – and dashing out their brains with his enormous stone patu. For years thereafter, my mother never had to worry about my absence from home once night fell.'[10]

In 1892 Jane returned with her family to Port Albert. The family lived in what had been the first store, just about ten feet from high water mark. A small jetty about a chain long ran out in front of the building, and every morning Jane's brother Bert would row across the river to work at his father's sawmill. But for Jane, who was now fifteen, there was little opportunity to do work other than to help her mother in the home. There was no hope of a secondary education for this bright intelligent young woman as there was no secondary school at Port Albert, and her being away from home to go to school was not a consideration. The tradition was for girls to stay at home with their mother, help at home, and wait to be married. Education was whatever could be snatched from the local school. For Jane, though, the lack of mental stimulation in things domestic was terrifying. Luckily the opportunity to become a pupil-teacher at Port Albert arose, and so Jane began her teaching career.

The headmaster at Port Albert then was George Reid; he had followed on from Benny Martin Gubb. George Reid had studied at the University of Edinburgh to become a Doctor of Medicine. However, he had a disagreement with his family and left England, and although he never completed his degree, he was an intelligent scholarly man. Jane stayed at the school, first as a pupil-teacher and then as an assistant teacher, until

1895. Pupil-teachers were rather like apprentices. They learned how to teach by teaching, and they were expected to pass Pupil Teacher's Examinations. In an extract from such an examination in 1908, more than ten years after Jane's training, but an exam which wouldn't have changed very much from when she sat it, the examinees were asked to 'Explain in detail how you would direct "Nature Study" of the oak tree'. The English influence in teacher training on New Zealand education is evident. Here was a school which was surrounded by bush, with kauri trees being milled, and the teachers, like their counterparts in England, were being examined on their observation of an oak tree. The text books used to teach the children were also those used by children in England. Books such as the *Nelson Royal Reader*, Gilkes' *Physical Geography*, and Creighton's *Rome* were all books with their origins firmly planted in English soil. New Zealand children were educated to be replicas of their English peers, with little attention being given to the natural world surrounding them. When considering the style of education available, it is perhaps even more surprising that Jane rose above this early educational doctrine and created something as original and so particularly New Zealand as *The Story of a New Zealand River*.

When Jane taught at Port Albert the roll was between fifty and sixty children, and the school room was very crowded. It was the same school she had attended as a child. The room was about 43 feet by 20 feet, and the children sat at desks, sometimes sharing one between two pupils, with all age groups catered for. Originally the building had a roof of wooden shingles, but this was replaced while Jane was there with corrugated iron. Although it meant a more sturdy roof, the noise when it rained was deafening. Outside in the playground was a shelter shed, where the children could play on wet days.

Jane's time as an assistant teacher at Port Albert ended when her father moved the family to a house in Avondale. Frank Mander had bought the timber rights in the upper Nihotupu Valley in 1895 from John Huston and Oliver Wasley, who owned the land. The kauri in Wasley's bush were magnificent, but had not previously been cut because of their remote location. Another problem apart from remoteness was the ruggedness of the landscape: the usual method of using a system of dams to drive the timber out was not possible here. However, Frank Mander's experience at Pukekaroro of building tramways was the answer to hauling out these formerly inaccessible kauri. Mander and Bradley set to work to build a four-kilometre tramway from the mill they had erected up in the Nihotupu. It must have been spectacular as it crossed over the Waitakere's present-day Scenic Drive ridge, down into the Henderson Valley.

Loads of sawn timber were winched up to the ridge near the site of the present television mast by a horse-powered capstan. They were then lowered down a series of steep inclines and over sixteen bridges to the floor of the Henderson Valley 300 metres below. From here the timber was loaded on wagons and hauled by traction engines to the Henderson Railway Station.[11]

While the family lived at Avondale Jane taught at a variety of Auckland schools: Devonport, Otahuhu, and Newton West. Newton West no longer exists, but both Devonport and Otahuhu schools are still educating Auckland children. While Jane was teaching, she also studied at night for her matriculation. This was essential for entry to the University of New Zealand, and in 1896 Jane passed in Latin, English, Arithmetic, Geometry, History, Geography, Mechanics and Chemistry. She was notified by the Registrar in February 1897 that she had passed. In a heavy bureaucratic tone she was also informed that:

> I am unable to give you information as to the number of Marks gained by you in any subject . Should you be a teacher wishing to obtain the D Certificate, I may tell you that the Education Department has been informed of your marks; but I can give you no further information on this subject.

Unfortunately the records relating to Jane's teaching career have been lost, so it is impossible to check on her exam results.

Jane was always regarded as a very proper teacher, but that didn't mean she was lacking in humour. The blue eyes would sparkle at the thought of some fun. Her brother Bert, in a little book of anecdotal stories, tells of how once when they were left alone at night in the house in Avondale he was woken by one of his younger sisters. She was frightened because she was sure someone was lying on the dining room floor. The Manders' house in Avondale was well back from the road and surrounded by trees and shrubbery, which made the interior very dark. Bert got Jane to come with him to the dining room.

> As we peered into the darkened room there was just enough light to see the figure which appeared to have slipped feet first under the table, the upper part of the body against the window seat. Long legs outlined from the shoes, clothes pushed up to the knees as would happen when slipping down and partly along the floor. Every appearance of collapse. One leg seemed to be grotesquely twisted over the other. My elder sister (Jane) hoarsely whispered to go and pull up the blind. While I was screwing up courage to do so with a vision of ghastly pallor and staring eyes – she dashed in and out again as the blind rattled up. I turned to look at her behind me to see her doubled up with laughter. One of the girls had evidently partly undressed there, pushed or kicked shoes off followed by stockings. A skirt next the window seat, while a cushion hanging over completed the illusion.

Bert ends his story by wondering if it had all been planned, and he was concerned that he had not cut a very heroic figure in front of his sisters. The prank may well have been planned, but whether it was or not, it is a telling gesture that it was Jane who had the courage to race into the room and pull up the blind. She never lacked courage and her fearlessness of public opinion was demonstrated much later in life when she took up the feminist cause in New York, and when she countered adverse criticism of her writing.

After teaching for eight years, Jane took a positive step toward realising her career as a novelist. In 1900 she retired from teaching. She would have made a magnificent headmistress, with her quick intellect, her humour, and her kindness. But while she taught she didn't write and it was writing that she wanted to do. She had always told stories, entertaining her brother and sisters on cold winter nights, but now she wanted to master the skill of putting a story on paper. Her story-telling skill was with her forever; as Olive de Malmanche said in later years, her children loved Jane Mander coming to baby-sit them as she always told them such wonderful stories.[12] Now she was going to work at a novel and try to become a published writer.

Frank Mander was on the move once again, but at last Jane would benefit from her father's need to find more work. Mander and Bradley were the successful bidders to cut timber at Puhi Puhi, about thirty miles north of Whangarei. They had paid the enormous sum of £5000 for the rights, but there was about 12 million super feet of kauri and totara, and they had eight years to remove the trees.[13] There was no need for the family to live close to the milling, and the Manders made Whangarei their home. After first renting somewhere to live, they moved into a house in Hatea Drive which Frank had built.

CHAPTER FOUR

≈

*Then her father bought a small country paper
and gave his daughter her first big chance.*
Freda Sternberg, *The Home*

Before Frank Mander built his house in Hatea Drive he bought, in partnership with Fred and Will Foote, the most prestigious paper in the North, the *Northern Advocate*. He had decided to enter into politics, and although his family thought him a 'silly old ass'[1] to contemplate election for a constituency where he was a newcomer, Frank was determined. He saw himself as something of a 'Timber King', as he now owned several timber mills in Northland. He wrote of himself, 'Mr Mander has not taken any active part in political or municipal affairs, although he is an enthusiastic member of the National Association, as his time has been fully occupied in fighting the battles of life; the only hobby he indulges in is the pursuit of art, and although he is not an artist by education, he has to some extent developed his artistic endowments'.[2] With the acquisition of the *Northern Advocate*, he had an organ which would present his own political views. In 1902 he contested the Marsden seat for the Reform Party against the sitting member Mr R. Thompson, and won the contest; he held the seat until his resignation at the end of 1922.

For Jane, her father's purchase of a newspaper meant there was an open door for her to pursue a career as a journalist. It would have been enormously difficult, otherwise, for a woman in the early 1900s to break into this male-dominated field. Her job was originally to be that of sub-editor, but she was also a reporter and general hand, and in a letter to Johannes Andersen in 1935 she says proudly, 'At times I ran the department single handed from leaders to proofs and the proudest boast of my life is that once I brought out the paper four days running without a mistake and caught the four o'clock train.'[3] Few newspapers today, even with their sophisticated, computerised equipment can echo that boast.

The house at Hatea Drive was built in 1905 and was the fulfilment of Frank Mander's desire for a grand home for his family. The timber for the house was barged from the Mander mill up the Hatea River to the house site. It was named 'Pukenui' after the hill behind the house. Ever thinking of his next challenge, Frank had designed and had built a house which would befit a Member of Parliament and a man of standing in the community. It was set on the edge of the town on several acres, with a background of native bush. There was a formal garden with a fountain, and at the gate were two sculpted figures; the driveway swept past the garden and round to the side of the house where there was a two-storied stable for the carriage and pair.[4] It is a pity, though, that Frank Mander had not bothered to ask his family for their opinion on the design. The big bow-windowed dining room was large enough to fit a twelve-foot dining table, and the fourteen foot eight inch stud gave the rooms a large airy feel, but the kitchen was small and dark and situated well away from the dining room. To get meals to the table even relatively warm was something which taxed the women of the house. There is a story which has circulated in the family that a neighbour would help out when there were important guests to dine by doing some of the cooking in their own kitchen and rushing the food across to the Mander home. On one occasion, the neighbour's child was delivering a hot cooked chicken to the Mander house when the guests started to arrive. The child had to hide in the bushes surrounding the garden, clutching the hot chicken until all the visitors were safely inside.

Later Jane would write articles on interior design, and in all her books the design of the interiors of houses is important. After years of living in houses which would be regarded now as sub-standard, she had developed a love for things of beauty to surround her. Beautiful paintings, books and china, and rooms which gave a feeling of serenity were important to her.

A special feature of the Hatea Drive house was its hexagonal gazebo on the roof. On one side was the door and the other walls were windowed. To gain access to the room there was a flight of stairs up the side of the house, a bit like a fire escape, and then a platform across the roof to the room. There was no internal access from the house. Jane claimed this as her writing room, and would disappear up to the roof-top room to work.

Arthur Pickmere bought the house from the Manders in 1912, and when he died it was inherited by his son Hereward, who had small children; the gazebo was removed from the roof as a safety measure and it sat in the garden for the children to use as a play-house. Later it was donated to the Northern Regional Museum and it can be seen in Whangarei at the Clarke Homestead, an historic house which is part of the museum complex. Nancy Pickmere, who was Hereward Pickmere's wife, thought the house was gloomy and said that she was very naughty and painted everything white including the kauri![5] The house, with reduced grounds

≈ Mander's Mill Dam on the Waiariki River, Puhipuhi, c. 1902, with bullock team in the foreground. Northern Advocate

≈ Top: The Mander Dam at Puhipuhi, after being tripped, c. 1902. Northern Advocate

≈ Bottom: Kauri logs at Whakapara, c. 1902. Northern Advocate

since the Mander's day, was until recently owned by another Member of Parliament, Mr John Banks. There have been modernisations in the kitchen and the bathrooms but the integrity of the house remains; it is still roomy and gracious, and the distinctive coloured square roof tiles have been maintained.

Knowing that she would not be disturbed, Jane would take herself to the room on top of the house and write. In 1902 she had a short story published in the *Illustrated Magazine* called 'A Stray Woman'. This is the earliest piece of her published work that has come to light. The story is a prosaic one of a woman who has not been treated well by a man:

> Dora Mortyn stood on the balcony beside her friend. A full moon was rising above some silver-tinged clouds in the east, and a beautiful long shimmer lay across Auckland Harbour in front of them. The two women revelled in the glory of it, and what was more, they both knew it without saying so. From the room behind them came sounds of loud laughter, for Mrs Allen Manston was telling the fortunes of the men who clustered around her. At an extra loud peal Dora turned to her friend and smiled. 'What a merry little soul she is,' she observed lightly.
>
> 'Er-yes. But it's a bit against the grain to see how readily our menfolk turn from our sensible conversation and rally round a frivolous toy like that,' answered the friend, a trifle bitterly.
>
> 'Oh it doesn't take much to amuse men,' said Dora with contempt.[6]

The dialogue is stilted and the story theme of a woman befriending a wife who is married to the man she once loved is flat and lacks any psychology, something that Jane was later to insist is important for writers to develop in their characters. It is the type of story which filled the pages of women's magazines at the time, and it is the only piece of writing where she uses her full name, Mary Jane Mander; nothing else she wrote was signed in that way. But it was a story published outside the confines of the *Northern Advocate*, so at last her career as a published writer had begun. She later said that she received no payment for the story but was happy to see something she had written appear in print.

Jane continued to work hard on her father's newspaper, but in 1906 she was tired, and unwell, and in need of a break. For the rest of her life, she would find that she could work hard for a period of time and then become so unwell that she would need to have a complete break in order to restore her health. Although she became known for her tremendous energy, that energy was not unlimited and she often pushed herself hard, only to suffer later.

So in 1907 Jane went to Sydney. Although Australia was New Zealand's nearest geographic neighbour, Sydney society was light-years away from anything Jane had experienced at home. At last she met other writers and artists, and was able to indulge her love of music by having some music lessons; she also studied French, and of course she wrote.

Jane came home to spend Christmas with her family at the end of 1907, but she was determined that she would return to Sydney. In order to make some money she took the job of editing the *North Auckland Times*, a newspaper produced in Dargaville. Nothing much relating to her stay in Dargaville remains. It has been said that at some stage files were burnt and papers were thrown into the river. However, she was able to use her experiences on the *North Auckland Times* as a basis for her novel *The Strange Attraction*. Included in the story is an election which could well have mirrored her father's election campaign in 1902; however, it is speculation and dangerous ground to start weaving a fictional story into the few known facts.

What is known for sure is that Jane was frustrated by the narrowness of the society in which she lived. This frustration is highlighted in a letter she wrote to *The Triad* in 1909. A monthly arts magazine, *The Triad* (1893-1927) was published in Dunedin. Later, during World War I, it moved to Sydney and was published there until it disappeared. Jane's feelings of constraint are obvious in this amusing and revealing letter:

> *Dear Triad*
>
> *I'm sorry you live in Dunedin, because if you were anywhere handy there are things I might mention. You have not deprived me critically of my 'presence' or my 'temperament' or my 'soul'. Don't keep such things in stock to be flattened, gold leaf-like under your Thorry touch. My only accomplishment is the joy of life, and that you have sadly marred. Where is my October Triad? Where is my Art Supplement?*
>
> *What have I ever done to the Triad but seize it from the post, and deserting all else, rejoice in it alone? Why the only thing that keeps me from preaching temperance, or making draughty garments for the superfluous heathen, or marrying a Sunday School teacher in this brain-benumbing, stimulus-stifling, sense-stultifying, soul-searing silence is the invasion of the Triad and its kind. Be good to me and send it on the Wings of a Wellington wind. And, please publish some more short poems by Oscar Wilde. And please take great care of Frank Morton.[7] There's a man I could live with and love, especially if he did the cooking. I live in hope of dining out with him some day. Then life in New Zealand would have produced the compensation. Don't die yet either of you. That Triad please. Yours in things worthwhile, J Mander, Whangarei.*

The restless tone of the letter is obvious from such words as 'brain-benumbing', 'stimulus-stifling', 'sense-stultifying'. Jane had tried to fill her time with intellectual pursuits – she had become a member of a debating team – but none of this was enough and she was restless; she wanted to be where there were other writers, other artists, where she could develop, and she was also aware that time was passing; she was thirty-three and still had not had a novel published. A rebellious, forthright and dynamic person, she could no longer sit at home in the rose-coloured drawing room helping to entertain her father's guests.

It was time to make a change, to be where she could absorb an artistic atmosphere, to study the craft of writing, and to move away from the meagre artistic diet she had in the North. In 1910 Jane went back to Sydney. This time she stayed with William Holman and his wife Ada.

CHAPTER FIVE

≈

*Until three years ago I knew
nothing of Socialism.*

Manda Lloyd/Jane Mander, *The Maoriland Worker*

It is not clear how Jane came to know the Holmans in Sydney but journalists do tend to flow together. It may well be that she had an introduction to them from her contacts with the *Northern Advocate*. There could not have been a more conducive environment for Jane's writing to blossom than in this household.

William Arthur Holman was to become in 1914 the first Labour Premier of New South Wales, but at this stage of his career he was working hard as a founder of the Labor Party. His wife Ada had been a Kidgell, with a father prominent in the literary and journalistic life of Victoria. Ada was a talented writer and became one of the most able of Australia's women journalists. Like Jane, she had worked as an editor and had superintended the printing of a newspaper. And also like Jane, Ada had an astringent wit, and had once published in the newspaper the following suggestions:

> 13. Borrow any of the editor's books you may care about. They are only kept for the purpose of being lent.
> 14. If you want your name printed in colours for nothing, you've only got to say so.
> 15. Borrow the foreman's bike whenever you want it, without asking; you'll find it outside.
> 17. Never call during office hours to pay accounts. Go to the reporter just before some meeting starts and ask him to come up to the office and give you 'that bill'.[1]

Ada Holman was deeply involved in the literary world in Sydney. She was also involved with the feminist movement and knew Rose Scott, a woman well known in Sydney circles for her pro-feminist views. The Holman household was an exciting entrance for Jane into the Sydney literary milieu.

Holman, who had worked as a cabinet-maker, saw and understood the difficulties of the working man. He had been appalled to discover the wage standard in New South Wales was so low. A skilled brick-maker worked for ten hours a day and received only seven shillings. A carpenter received as little as nine shillings a day and the engineering tradesman as little as ten shillings, also for a ten-hour day.[2] He saw that the way to make changes was not through strike action but through legislation. It was with this in mind that he set about working to establish the Labor Party.

Into this environment of concern and activity came Jane. As well as writing and studying, she continued with her piano lessons and became good enough to play for friends, but not good enough to become a concert pianist – that would have to remain an unredeemed dream. However, she was able to transfer that dream to Asia in *The Story of a New Zealand River*, for Asia becomes a well-known pianist when she goes to Sydney.

After living in the remote areas of the North, with the largest town having a population of 5000 people, the busyness of Sydney must have had a huge impact on Jane. She was able to study and write in an environment where intellectual discussion took place, and where contact with other artists was possible. Sydney also had its own publishing houses. In New Zealand, any manuscript had to be sent overseas for a publisher to consider – usually to London. By the time a manuscript reached England there was no one to promote the work or the author, and there the book would languish. Here, at least, Jane could talk to people who were in the publishing world about books and about writing – the whole artistic atmosphere was far removed from the isolation and remoteness she experienced in New Zealand.

However, because she had lived in remote bush areas where survival often depended on the help of a neighbour, Jane understood the virtue of hard work, often for small recompense. She had a sympathy for the underdog and the underprivileged and was ripe to be influenced by the Holmans' views on socialism. Under the pseudonym of Manda Lloyd. she wrote an article entitled 'A Woman's View' for *The Maoriland Worker*, supporting social revolution:

> Until three years ago I knew nothing of Socialism, I was entirely in sympathy with all the people who worked, for I had worked myself, had been poor enough to go to bed in the dark to save candles, had owned but one pair of shoes at a time, etc. My environment improved considerably, but I realised that I was still up against forces that hampered my individuality; that things were all wrong somehow. Still, I had not begun to think economically. I learnt of reform, not of revolution. I heard casually of Socialism as a ridiculous fad, and for some time thought nothing of it. Still I knew capitalism was wrong, and I hated the spirit of it. Then three years ago in Sydney, I heard Socialism preached for the first time. I had only to realise it to believe in it, to know that it was what I had groped towards.[3]

Why the *nom de plume*? Many writers use different names for different publications, but at the time that Jane was writing this article for *The Maoriland Worker* her father was M.P. for Marsden in the Reform Party, a party which had nothing in common with socialism. The Reform Party saw itself as anti-socialist, meaning that it resisted wage increases, tax increases, and any nationalising schemes which may or may not threaten property rights, particularly in country areas. It was a party which admired the man who made his way in the world, who was a success through hard work. Most of the leading Reformers were like Frank Mander himself, self-made men. In 1912 the Reform Party became the Government. It was probably in deference to her father's position as an M.P. for a party with nothing in common with a socialist revolution, that Jane announced her birth as a Socialist under a different name.

Another article by Jane which also appeared in *The Maoriland Worker* was entitled 'The Children's Court – The Problem of the Neglected and the Unwanted Child'. She was enormously fond of children; Ron Holloway tells a story of Jane coming to visit after she returned to New Zealand in the thirties. She gave him money to buy the children strawberries, because she said it was important that children learn about things other than the prosaic. He was not to spend the money on shoes. As she left the Holloway house she stood at the gate and called back to Ron and Kaye Holloway in her very loud voice, 'Remember not shoes, strawberries!'

The article uses the picture of children who wash up in the children's court to emphasise the necessity of having a contraceptive programme, and even borders on the suggestion of euthanasia.

> I entered the Children's Court in Sydney full of hope and curiosity. Here surely there were opportunities of dealing sanely with the problem of children mentally morally and physically diseased. I was intensely eager to see what a department that claims to be one of the most progressive in the world was doing for these loose ends of humanity. On a platform at the end of a table sat a benign old fossil, whose prehistoric limitations became evident as the morning proceeded – a nice, earnest old man, with a sublime childlike faith in the efficacy of a parrot-like knowledge of the ten commandments and the multiplication table.[4]

The story continues with three examples of young boys brought before the court for minor demeanours such as swearing in a public place, stealing carrots and parsnips from a Chinaman's garden, and travelling on a tram without paying. In each case the children are asked if they know the Ten Commandments and their multiplication tables. The ridiculousness of the whole system is pointed out by Jane, but her major polemic is left to the end of the article.

There will always be thousands of unwanted children under the capitalist system. We shall never have quality until we can have homes that are *homes*, the outward expression of the love that two happy people bear each other. When normal people are happy and comfortable and not demoralised by the fear of unemployment, they want children who are most valuable to the State, but it is impossible for any human being to desire to bring helpless creatures into a world that can give them nothing but cruel struggle and inevitable degradation; and I say that if the modern State cannot or will not alter these wretched conditions under which the poor live its obvious duty is to spread the knowledge that will prevent births at all under such crippling circumstances. Bonuses for large families, indeed! I think of all the ridiculous things ever suggested by man this is the most futile! I should like to know if one child anywhere on earth has been born as the result of the alluring offer of £5 per head.[5]

She saved her most controversial idea until the last paragraph when she said,

And there won't be any fossils because in a sane state the fossil will be the unpardonable sin, and directly he shows signs of arriving he will be given a good dinner and lulled into eternal sleep with the latest anaesthetic.[6]

The Holman household was like a whirlpool, their contacts with journalists and writers being not merely confined to the Sydney scene. People from many parts of the world visited them.

It was in this world of writers, artists and musicians that Jane heard of the Journalism School at Columbia University in New York. American friends of the Holmans convinced Jane that this was the place which allowed women freedom to pursue a career, that if writing was what she wanted to do it would be the place to study. She had been offered a scholarship in German at the University in Sydney, but she turned it down and decided she would return to New Zealand. There she would try to persuade her family to help her fulfil her ambition of getting to New York to attend Barnard College at Columbia University.

The arguments about Jane going overseas raged. When she was in New York some years later she wrote an article entitled 'Sheltered Daughters', which was published in *The New Republic* on 24 June 1916. Jane rails against the common assumption as to what comprised a daughter's duty. The article begins:

The sheltered daughter is to be found in all kinds of homes where economic pressure has not found its way. She is one of the crimes for which poverty is not responsible. She may be preserved for various ends, of which the three most clearly defined are the marriage market, safety in the hands of the Lord, and the comfort and use of her parents.

As she expounds her theory she says of the daughter who is bred for the 'comfort and use of her parents':

> And thirdly there is the daughter who is regarded as the special property of her parents, who is bred to be their comfort and companion. If she hints at a desire to earn her own living, the 'bond' and 'filial duty' are preached to her as something that should be sacred beyond question. She is expected to stay at home and prove her gratitude for the sacrifices that have been made for her. Her natural inclination to love and trust her parents is exploited to the full.

With a tenacity probably inherited from her father, Jane eventually got her own way. She arrived in London in the summer of 1912. The two months spent in London were everything she had imagined that great city could offer. England was still referred to as 'Home' by many New Zealanders, and Jane did feel at home there, but her ultimate goal was New York. So in September she left London and the friends she had made on the ship, to sail to the metropolis which extended promises of glittering success.

Chapter Six

≈

*Before I had been very long at the University
I was quite a pet, as I was the first
New Zealand student to go there.*
Talk given to the Lyceum Club, 1933

Though Jane had broken away from the backblocks of New Zealand and had experienced life in cities the size of Sydney and London, nothing had prepared her for the impact of New York. As the ship steamed past the Statue of Liberty and up to the docks on the Hudson River, the reflection of the sun on the buildings created the appearance of a golden city. Even in 1912 the city was reaching for the sky. The Flatiron building built in 1903 was ninety-one metres high, and an eighteen-storey skyscraper was being built to replace the old Cotton Exchange in the heart of the financial district.[1] She found the city noisy and tiring and at first kept away from the centre of the city and stayed close to the University.

Jane's destination on arrival was uptown Manhattan, to 116th Street West. The women's college of Barnard was situated across the road from the great university of Columbia. It was at Barnard that Jane was to prepare for her entry into the journalism course at Columbia.

In 1903 Joseph Pulitzer donated money toward setting up a journalism school at Columbia. It had taken longer to implement than had first been anticipated. However, the president of Columbia, Dr Nicholas Murray Butler, was keen to have the school and hoped that it would be a first in the country, but he wanted it to be set up in the usual classical academic style. He felt it was important that a new course such as journalism should remain within the usual university structure. This was where the arguments arose with Pulitzer, and so there were delays in getting the school underway. Pulitzer insisted that the school should keep one foot in the highway of events – this was one reason why he had chosen Columbia, as it had a reputation of being a forward-looking college. Pulitzer, who suffered from ill health, had his physician write to Dr Butler, insisting that there must be admission for students without previous collegiate credits. 'Upon any other basis, there would have been excluded from such a school nearly every distinguished journalist I ever knew. Mr. Pulitzer could not have been admitted, nor could Mr. James Gordon Bennet, neither the first nor the second, nor Horace Greeley, nor the earliest and most famous of our newspaper men, Ben Franklin himself.'[2]

Not only did it take longer to set up the School of Journalism than was first envisaged, but it was also a long time before the university authorities at Columbia agreed to allow women to enter the course. When finally it did open its doors to women it was the first of the professional schools at Columbia to do so. It took the Law and Medical faculties much longer to agree to have women students.

It was by a last-minute compromise with Barnard College that an agreement was reached with Columbia. The college would undertake the two years of collegiate preparation for women, who would then join the men for professional subjects.[3] Barnard had the happy knack of finding scholars of great distinction to teach their students – two such men were Professor James Harvey Robinson and Professor John Bates Clark. The college agreed to release these men to teach at Columbia and in return it secured the admission of women to graduate courses in the journalism faculty. These negotiations were still going on when Jane was on her way to America, but for once in her education luck was on her side. By the time she arrived at the college, the path had been prepared for women to attend the journalism course at Columbia after they had finished their preparatory work at Barnard. She was to maintain later that it was because of New Zealand's lead in social legislation that the entrance rules were altered specially for her:

> When I first went to New York to Columbia University I was astonished to find myself regarded as an 'event of importance' the first New Zealander to enter there as a student. I was an 'object of inspiration' and was subjected to exhaustive questioning because of the excitement over what my country 'stood for'. We were then leaders in social legislation! We were high minded about the value of human life! We were socialism without bloodshed! We were Utopia materialised! Yes all that. A positively exciting country! And its glory reflected itself on me, and I became a university pet, and even the entrance rules were amended to meet my 'case' such was the enthusiasm.[4]

It is doubtful that the entrance rules were amended specifically for Jane, but she did come into the category which Pulitzer had insisted upon, and it is likely that consideration was given to the fact that not only had she worked as a teacher, but she had also worked as an editor on a newspaper. At last things were starting to fall into place for her.

Jane's arrival at Barnard came close on the heels of the famous Dean, Miss Virginia Gildersleeve. Miss Gildersleeve, who was the same age as Jane, became Dean in 1911, but her journey to Barnard couldn't have been more dissimilar to that of Jane. Miss Gildersleeve came from a family who not only valued education but insisted upon it. Her father was a New York supreme court justice, and when the President of the University, Dr Nicholson Butler, told Justice Gildersleeve that he intended to make Virginia the dean, Justice Gildersleeve replied 'I'm not surprised. Virginia will make you a good dean'. Nobody has been able to say truthfully in the thirty-five years she served that her father was mistaken.[5] In later times, Miss Gildersleeve remembered Jane Mander well, partly because Jane was an older student, but also because of her striving for academic excellence in all her courses.

As a non-matriculated special student Jane found her academic work-load at Barnard heavy. To be accepted into the journalism course at Columbia meant that she must have an academic record of high standing. She studied English, French, History, Science, Philosophy and Politics, and in her exams got As in every subject except History, where she scored the only B in the whole of her academic career. At the end of her first year there is a note on her record to say that 'The question of additional credit for high standing will be determined by the School of Journalism when your Barnard College work is finished. Barnard College will then report to the School of Journalism what credits you would have had if you had registered as a regular.' Jane was proving her ability in academic work and was to write later in 1913 that she had done rather brilliantly in her exams, and had gained the highest possible mark in all subjects, but was weary afterwards. In her first semester she did little other than study hard, but she had hardly any money and less time. She did not take part in any of the extra-curricular activities Barnard was famous for, and does not appear in any of the Mortarboard publications of the college. She was too busy to write for that publication, and may well have thought that many of the activities which the younger students enjoyed and entered into were too juvenile for her. Instead she revelled in the big libraries at the university, and the lounges which overlooked the river. She did manage to get to the Opera, and was overwhelmed with the magnificence of it all.

They don't lie when they say it's the finest in the world. It certainly licks London. The staging is simply indescribably sumptuous, and the music beyond one's dreams.

What happened for Jane at Barnard was what she had dreamed of when she was writing to *The Triad* back in 1910. It had happened in part in Sydney when she met with writers and artists there, but here in New York she was in much more international company. For the first time she was surrounded by an intellectual stimulation which provided all the pleasure and delight she needed. 'Have got to know two or three groups of fascinating people. One Bohemian set of lawyers, writers artists etc. all I want in the way of diversion.[6]

Before she left New Zealand, Jane had decided that if she booked a room in one of the great dormitories of the university she would not be lonely. On arrival however, she was staggered by the size of Whittier Hall. It was a great E-shaped building of twenty storeys and there were nine hundred women living in it. She certainly wasn't going to be lonely. 'The first girl I spoke to in the building, a stranger like myself, had come from Honolulu, and just before had taken a trip out to New Zealand and had been entertained in Auckland by friends of mine – who had been almost the last people I had seen before leaving New Zealand myself'.[7] According to Jane, Whittier Hall was a great gaol-like place of steel and concrete, with gloomy long grey corridors, with not a thing in them. The rooms were small and initially she wondered how she would ever stand hers as it was situated next to the lift. However, she later managed to get a better room in a quieter part of the Hall. Despite the smallness of the rooms and the utilitarian feel of the place, there were small human touches which made the welcome warm even if the building itself was forbidding. For instance, when each woman arrived and registered at the desk she was asked when her birthday was, so in April when it was Jane's birthday her table with eight women was given a special birthday dinner with a birthday cake with seventeen candles, and flowers, and a New Zealand flag stuck in the middle. As this happened for every foreign student in the dormitory, there were birthday parties every week.

Jane was initially impressed with the thoughtfulness of the administration at Whittier. She says, 'I found at my first dinner in that house, sweet potatoes. They had actually taken the trouble to find out that there were sweet potatoes in New Zealand, and as America grows them as well (very few countries do) they had thought I might like to see something native. And they took this trouble to provide some homelike food for all the non-Americans, and this in a building of nine hundred women, and in a University having at that time some 24,000 students enrolled'.[8] Later, though, the institutional food became tedious and she says that 'in the course of time everybody got acclimatised to the American food, which was scientifically portioned out in Calories, quite enough to support hard working students, but not enough to produce extra fat.' She also found that they were not allowed a rebate if they did not eat at the dining room, and wanted to eat somewhere else for a change. As her money was very tight, she was unable to eat out and had to accept the monotony of the food. Later however, she talks of 'a rich girl next me who is always giving me fruit and candies, and others who have taken me out to dinners and afternoon teas in swell places.'[9]

Not all the women who were living at Whittier Hall were attending Barnard. Many were studying at what was called Teachers' College, which was a technical and classical college combined. It was a college which taught everything – business management, book-keeping, millinery design, house decorating, cabinet making, publicity drawing and poster design and advertising. This meant there was an enormous cross-section of women, from all parts of the state as well as from varied backgrounds. Jane made many good friends, friends who stayed with her all her life. She was older than the majority of the women, and her experience, good sense, and humour endeared her to people. She became a sort of elder sister to many of the young women she met, and was always a good confidante as she never gossiped.

By the greatest good fortune Jane happened to attend Barnard at the same time as two women who were to become her life-long friends, and who welcomed her into their family as their own. Esther and Rose Norton came from a wealthy New York family and it was through the Nortons that Jane met many of the influential and interesting people in New York. The Nortons were enormously generous to Jane. They would invite her to stay with them and often handed on clothing which they thought would be useful to her. She was never too proud to accept the clothing or the meals and in return they all received the most wonderful friendship from Jane. Her kindness was unbounded – Esther Norton Soule once said that you didn't know anything about friendship until you had met Jane Mander.

Esther remembered Jane as very reserved on personal matters and very uncomplaining:

> She talked in a vigorous decisive (rather controversial) manner, very positive about her own opinions, but I always knew she was good-natured underneath this brusque speech. She rather liked to sound like a Shavian heroine, unsentimental and harsh, a non-conformist, but she was really very tender. She encouraged me to be a modern woman! – career, suffrage, literary ambition etc.[10]

In Jane's novel *The Besieging City*, the heroine Christine Mayne has some of the attributes Esther Norton saw in Jane. In particular the heroine has a reticence about all things personal:

> Most girls wanted friendship to be an eternal confessional. They wanted to know all about you. They had no conception of intimacy apart from the revelation of secrets. Their idea of friendship was that nothing was kept back. Brought up in an entirely different tradition, and being by temperament aloof, Chris knew she was much misunderstood, and was now resigned to the fact.

Of all her friends only Julia Hayden and Ellis Mair had her own feeling about this. With them she had never discussed purely personal matters. She had not the faintest idea of the secrets of their lives, nor had she ever wondered what they might be. She had come to feel that the revelation of secrets added little to one's appreciation of a person. Like Redman she preferred to know people through imagination. She wished her friends to make a picture of themselves, and then to preserve that picture from smudges.... Of all the unpardonable sins a vulgar curiosity was to Chris the most obnoxious.[11]

Later, when Jane became friendly with Monroe Wheeler and Glenway Wescott (who were homosexuals), she burnt their letters to her as she believed they were private and for her eyes only.

Esther and Rose's parents were also fond of Jane, as she was of them, and they agreed to allow Esther to share a flat with Jane when she left Whittier Hall and went to live in Morningside Drive. Later in the summer of 1914 Jane went with Rose and Esther to France to act as their chaperone, although there is a story that Jane left Rose and Esther at a chateau and then took off to Paris on her own. However, they were all together in Tours when war broke out and they stayed there for ten days waiting for news. The only place where they could get any information was at the Mayor's office, where news sheets were posted. The rumours grew with lightning speed, but Jane's determination and perseverance eventually secured them a booking on a ship to return to the United States via London.

Jane became enormously impressed at the quickness of American girls at learning. She maintained that the American business girl was the best educated girl of her type she had ever met. As an example she was impressed with her hairdressers in New York, who were women interested in things outside their shop-work. They read some of the same books that she read and could discuss them intelligently with her, they went to plays and were interested in countries outside of the U.S.A. Comparing them later with their London counterparts, she wrote that the women she went to in that city were only interested in adornment, in being made up like a doll, and making money. Obviously there was no intellectual exchange when she had her hair done in London. As well as being impressed by their intelligence and ability to experience and try new things, Jane also thought that American women dressed better than anyone she had ever seen, although she based this opinion on the women she saw in New York. All these attributes fitted in well with her own outlook and so she blossomed. Writing back to Tommy she says,

Nothing could describe the adorableness of American women and girls. Their goodness to me is just overwhelming. I really love the life as I have

≈ TOP: THE MANDER HOME AT HATEA DRIVE, WHANGAREI, IN 1906. THE GAZEBO, WHERE JANE USED TO WRITE, HAS SINCE BEEN REMOVED. WHANGAREI MUSEUM

≈ BOTTOM: JANE MANDER (LEFT) WITH MISS MARSHALL (CENTRE) AND MISS V. HOSKING, AT HATEA DRIVE C. 1908-09. THE ARCHWAY WAS A WHALE'S JAWBONE, COVERED WITH A CLIMBER. WHANGAREI MUSEUM

≈ TEA AND BISCUITS: MISS V. HOSKING (LEFT) AND JANE MANDER, C.
1908-09. WHANGAREI MUSEUM

≈ JANE MANDER (CENTRE) WITH MISS V. HOSKING (LEFT) AND MISS
MARSHALL AT THE BACK OF THE MANDER HOME IN HATEA DRIVE,
WHANGAREI. WHANGAREI MUSEUM

≈ A BUSH PICNIC, C. 1910. JANE MANDER IS SEATED SECOND ON RIGHT.
WHANGAREI MUSEUM

never loved anything else, altho' I'm dashed hard up. I've very little above my board and fees left over. But I'll manage somehow.[12]

Although she had bought clothes in London hoping that they would last her while she was in New York, it was obvious to her that this would not be the case. Moreover, she could certainly not afford anything like the clothes she saw other women wearing. A coat in corduroy, not really warm enough for a New York winter, could cost from $19.75 to $25.00. In an advertisement in the New York Times for Glubel's millinery, 'Hats in the Medium Price Salon were from $6.75 – $14.75 in the French Salon $15.00 – $150.00 and for Paris Modes up to $300.00'. Even the modest price of $6.75 was well out of Jane's price range. She complained to Tommy that it cost her 4/- to 5/- per week to have her washing done in the summer. She wore crepe so as not to need ironing, and she chose dark colours, but as she says

> *...one cannot live in navy blue when everybody else is in white. The Americans have shoes and stockings to match every dress they wear. They dress beautifully but frightfully extravagantly. These girls have already given me two dresses, some shoes and stockings, and odds and ends. They dress pretty well, and I have only the plainest of things. Clothes are the most appalling price.*

There is a comment about wearing handed-on clothing in *The Besieging City* when Chris Mayne visits the Hamiltons for a musical evening;

> She looked at herself in a long mirror. Blue did suit her. She hoped nobody would remember that half the dress she was wearing had been taken from one Ada had given her a year before. Fortunately Ada wore clothes for so short a time that the chance of their being recognised even by relatives was reduced to a minimum.[13]

Another friend Jane had made at Barnard was Katherine Davis and it was with the Davis family that Jane spent some of the summer in 1913. Like the Nortons, the Davises were delighted that their daughter had Jane as a friend. Kathy Davis was clever but unstable; but it seemed that Jane had the ability to soothe her. Before exams Kathy became ill with nerves and it was Jane who would walk with her and talk to her and rub her head until she went to sleep. Kathy became devoted to Jane, and all her family and friends noticed the difference in her under Jane's influence. It seemed that Jane had the ability to calm Kathy, who for no apparent reason would descend into the most hysterical white rages. Kathy's family were relieved that here at last was someone whose good sense and serenity made such an impact on her during her periods of irascibility. Interestingly she never took her rages out on Jane, and Jane in her turn found Kathy fascinating and unusual. She was a talented singer and whistler, and could play the guitar expertly, and some nights in the tent, she would play the guitar until Jane fell asleep.

Jane had finished her exams and was exhausted from her hard academic efforts, but despite her tiredness she was hoping to get back to work on her book, and needed somewhere congenial to work. The invitation from Kathy Davis to spend the summer at Lake George came at the perfect time. The Davises were not wealthy, Jane described them as 'sort of genteel keeping up appearances'. But they had a lovely place on Lake George, where they put up a tent for her to write in and left her to get on with her work. The tent was very different from the tents Jane had camped in back in New Zealand, and even more removed from the sort of tents in which her mother had made their home in the early days at bush camps.

This tent was 16 x 16 and fully, not to say elaborately, furnished. There was carpet on the floor and three standard lamps, afternoon tea china, and it was all painted and upholstered in a dark green. Jane delighted in the artistic look of it all. Both women had large lounge chairs, which had eight large cushions again in the dark green, and across the front of the tent was an eight-foot veranda with a hammock and rocking chairs on it. It was a comfortable and quiet place for Jane to write. She was intrigued that the whole household respected her wish to work on her book and took pains to leave her to get on with her work and not disrupt her inspirations. Soon Jane was able to say to Tommy,

> I've got my book nearly all done. I like it better now myself, and I hope I shall get it off this time. I shall have to type the alterations when I get back to New York.[14]

It is likely that the book she was working on was a rewrite of the work she had submitted to Heinemann's in London. It is unlikely that it was *The Story of a New Zealand River*, for this was still to come. There is no further mention or any record of this manuscript.

The holiday at Lake George was of enormous value to Jane. She admitted that she had put on some weight – because she often couldn't afford to eat properly she was nearly always underweight. She could write all day if she wished, but she was also having fun. She played tennis on the Davis's court, and went out on the lake in the boats that were available. After her hard grind at university, and her lack of money to do anything special in New York, this holiday in the land of millionaires was, as she said, the 'most glorious I have ever had'. Apart from the holiday aspect, though, Jane was looking at what was happening around her with her novelist's eyes. In her book *The Besieging City* many of the people she encountered on her holiday emerge to take up their positions as characters. These were wealthy cultivated and sophisticated people, their lives far removed from the kauri forests and the bush mill towns where she had grown up.

CHAPTER SEVEN

≈

In August every available person was mobilized.

Carrie Chapman Catt: A Biography[1]

By the end of 1914 Jane had moved out of the barracks – like Whittier Hall and was living in a small apartment at Janus Court, 106 Morningside Drive. It was within walking distance of Barnard, and she described it as looking nice. She had rented it furnished and it pleased her that Miss Hill, her landlady, had such good taste. She added some bookshelves of her own and was happy that she had such an attractive place to live.

Again Jane set about working hard at her studies and again she achieved top marks in every subject. At the same time, she continued to write articles. To Tommy she writes,

> *I've made a little money by odd writing jobs which has helped me make up the difference [of money]. I thought the third year's course would be easier, but it's worse. However, I love the life.*

Jane's study timetable, which she stuck to assiduously, left her little time to enjoy the entertainments New York had to offer. Also her lack of money meant she had to forgo the available joys of music and theatre. However, she did go one night to Carnegie Hall as a guest of Esther Norton to hear an orchestral concert, preceded by a turkey dinner at the Nortons'. A millionaire uncle of Esther had booked four boxes for the large party in which Jane was included to hear his protégée play with the orchestra – he had paid for a girl from one of his works to go to Germany for four years to study music, and this was the night of her début.

Jane was delighted to be invited, not only for the enjoyment of the music, but also for the amusement she had from the 'swell' company in the boxes:

> *Esther and Rose Norton and I did not go in evening dress (I don't possess any) but all the others did. There were two millionaires and their wives there, a wretched, shallow, jealous nervous looking lot of women. Mrs Norton herself is lovely, and a perfect dear, but some of her relatives are awful. Mad I call them. I can't endure them but I enjoyed the concert and the box. New*

York goes on just the same in spite of the war. Indeed there's more on here than ever, because the singers and plays [sic] have fled from Europe.[2]

With the prospect of America entering the war, Jane and Esther would get wildly excited about the war news. They both became notorious in the dining room for arguing with everybody. In her usual fashion Jane read everything she could about the war and was interested in the political situation in both America and England. She was proud that she could out-argue just about anyone on the various facts relating to the war. With her ability to marshall facts and figures, and a voice which was dominant, there were few who could counter her arguments!

Jane's lecturer in politics at Barnard was Charles Austin Beard. In 1914 he wrote a book called *An Economic Interpretation of the Constitution of the United States* which was regarded as controversial. Later in 1917 he resigned from Columbia in protest over two colleagues who had been dismissed. That he did not agree with the views of those who were dismissed was irrelevant, as he thought they had been badly treated. After he resigned he set up the New School for Social Research in New York. A radical with such high ideals and with such a humanitarian outlook was always going to have a receptive audience in Jane. In 1915 an article by Charles Beard supporting women's suffrage was published in the *New Republic*.

> When we see the question of woman suffrage in its proper perspective and an inevitable product of growing democracy, as a part of that long battle of common humanity against superiorities, royal, feudal, and masculine, we begin to see a new light, we begin to see why it is that women in the long run are destined to win. The fatal error was made when they were taught to read and write and the gateways to knowledge were opened to them. It is now too late to turn back the hands of the clock. They will penetrate the 'mysteries' of masculine government, just as the common man penetrated the 'mysteries' of royal government. They know more now and are better prepared for the ballot by far than the common man was when he received it.

Looking at this portion of the article it is easy to see that Jane and Charles Beard would have much in common and become friends, and it is interesting to note that the tone of the piece is similar to writing Jane was also doing for the *New Republic*. After just two years, Jane was now in the midst of an intellectual group writing for a new paper which was acquiring prestige with each issue. Her success is impressive in a city as cynical and as difficult as New York. It says much for her intellectual abilities as well as for her other personal attributes of good humour and directness, that she became not only accepted by such a group but sought after.

For Jane the summer of 1915 was as far removed from her summer with the Davis family as could possibly be imagined. Jane says that 'somebody told the suffrage leader Mrs Carrie Chapman Catt about me'.[3] Mrs Chapman Catt was leading the campaign for the first New York referendum on woman suffrage, 1915. The campaign had started in the previous January and she was working hard at organising women to vote for the referendum in November of 1915. Despite the fact that there was a major war taking place which tended to overshadow everything else, Mrs Chapman Catt was determined to keep the issue of votes for women in the public eye: 'She swore that neither things present nor things to come should hold the cause back now that its time had come to move.'[4]

Jane had been working hard at her writing, trying to get work accepted by various journals and magazines. She realised that not only did speaking for suffrage fit in with her own beliefs – after all New Zealand women had been voting at the polls for the past twenty-three years, but it was also a way of advertising herself. 'I really did it for the advertisement. You're nowhere in America if you're not known, and speaking is a quick way to get known.'[5] With her clear loud voice she soon became known as one of the best speakers in New York. She wasn't nervous and she was known to be eloquent and amusing:

> Father would be scandalised if he knew the street meetings I have addressed, standing on the proverbial soapbox, or on the seats of motor cars. I've often wished my family could see me. But keep it dark. Everybody does it here, from wealthy and famous women downwards, so it's nothing in these parts. I love the street meetings – it's amazing how the crowds are and my voice is an asset. I've one of the best carrying voices in the party for street speaking, and, as I say nothing gets you known quicker.[6]

Jane's father may have been shocked at his eldest daughter's street corner meetings, but he may well have understood that as well as putting forward the case for women to have the vote, she was working hard at getting herself known. After all, to further his own parliamentary hopes he had bought a newspaper.

Her loud voice, which was remembered by many of her friends, was not always appreciated by everyone. Rangi Cross, her nephew, remembers walking down Queen Street in Auckland with Aunt Jane when he was about eleven. She spoke all the time to him, making comments about the people and the things about them in a voice which carried for all to hear. As any eleven year-old would be, he was mortified with embarrassment.[7]

The first semester for 1915 had finished. Jane thought she would probably have to spend the summer in the soaring temperatures of the city. However, Miss Hill her landlady, who was a keen suffragist, and who had money and some good ideas to go with the money, had decided on a plan. She found an old hotel at Trenton Falls in Utica County which she could use free of charge for two months. Her idea was to combine a holiday in the country for New York children between the ages of twelve and fifteen, who would otherwise never get out of the city, with a suffragist programme of meetings and speaking engagements in that area. For her manager of provisions she chose her lodger Jane. It was a paid job and would help Jane pay for her next semester.

> *I am to have my mornings entirely to myself and Miss Hill has bought me a lovely new tent, fitted up with bed, chairs, table, floor etc. which I'm to have all to myself. She's great on suffrage and has always liked me. You can't beat Americans if they like you. They will do most amazing things for you, if they have the money. I'm really looking forward to getting into the country, and I guess I'll get some fun out of the wild experiment as we call it.*[8]

It was as if the Good Fairy had waved her wand. Jane could get out of the confines of the city and its high temperatures. She would have some company for some of the time but would also have privacy and a chance to write each day. She would do some speaking at the suffragist meetings, and so have her name mentioned in the newspapers, and as well she would be paid a wage. It suited her perfectly.

'The Wild Experiment' was written up in the *Utica Daily Press* on 28 July 1915. No advertising agency could have thought up a better advertising campaign for suffrage than this idea of Miss Hill's.

> Suffrage is not the whole thing, so far as the workers at Trenton Falls are concerned, and this will be demonstrated to many from Utica and the northern towns of Oneida County who take part in the meeting there today. They will find an enterprise which is providing a vacation for New York youngsters and school training for them and other activities which indicate the versatility of those who are interested in votes for women. New York City teachers are giving themselves to suffrage in many and various ways to win the state for votes for women at the November election. It remained for Miss Cora M. Hill however, to devise a scheme for combining vacation, charity and suffrage in one enterprise which is bringing health and happiness to herself and some fellow-teachers, helping forty children to a grand good time in the country, and furnishing a stronghold from which the battle for enfranchisement of women can be waged throughout that particular countryside.

Jane's speech on the situation of women and the social climate in New Zealand was given large coverage in the newspaper the following day:

> Miss Mander of New Zealand who is staying at the inn and lending her assistance in the work for the little girls and the suffrage cause was then introduced. Miss Mander told what suffrage has done in New Zealand. She

spoke of the strangeness of the attitude of men and women toward the question with the arguments against sex war, rivalry, etc. She said that where she had lived with men and women on an equal basis, there were no such things nor were they ever thought of. She first refuted arguments that have been advanced in this country. The demoralization of the standards of men or women she denied and gave proof of her statements .... The wonderful thing in Miss Mander's address was her story of the enforcement of the laws. That the laws are enforced regardless of the wealth or position of the offender seems incredible to Americans. Miss Mander was very emphatic about this fact, and gave instances of the support of women of this branch of the government.[9]

Following that address Jane then travelled with Miss Hill to meet up with Mrs Chapman Catt for a conference at Utica. And before she returned to New York she went north to Rome to make speeches, because the organisation in Rome had asked specifically for her. She was treated enormously well – like a visiting dignitary – put into the best hotel and with a motor car at her disposal. She made four speeches while she was there and met, as she says 'many charming people'. Despite becoming very tired toward the end of the summer experiment, Jane had found the suffrage lecture work fun. It also meant she had at last managed to position herself in New York with good contacts. Many of the women involved with the suffrage movement were wealthy, and Jane got to know Mrs O.H.P. Belmont, one of New York's social leaders, who also wanted her to speak during the suffrage campaign. These women had influence not only through their husbands but in their own right, and they were happy to help this woman from New Zealand with the loud voice and the fascinating accent, who could pull a crowd when she spoke.

Back at Morningside Drive in September Jane wrote to Tommy:

> Our hotel-camp-picnic turned out very well on the whole. The girls loved it, and were vastly improved in mind, body, and soul. But there was an awful lot of work. I came back here to find myself famous for my management, and I got an awfully nice send-off a week ago from the servants, and the girls and the staff. As Miss Hill and some others were away on a four days trip with the motor car, I had to walk two and a half miles to [the] railway station, and all the girls in their camp rig, with staffs and feathered heads, and all the remaining teachers, and several boarders, and two men escorted me to the station and gave the camp rally, etc. It was awfully nice. I'm sure everybody on the train thought we were mad. But Americans are perfectly lovely in that way. They are like a lot of kids.[10]

The final feature of the suffrage campaign in New York was the parade up Fifth Avenue on Saturday 23 October:

The day was sunny and cold. The bugle sounded at one o'clock, and the head of the column started from Washington Arch northward. At the head, following the platoon of mounted police and the mounted suffrage guard of honor, walked Mrs Catt, accompanied by national officers and the Empire State Campaign Committee. Then came organization after organization of women carrying their colors, carrying flags, carrying banners with inscriptions, with bands playing. Every county, every city in the state was there represented. The other campaign states sent delegations. They poured out of the side streets into the avenue to take their appointed places in the column as it came along. When Mrs Catt reached Central Park, she hastened back to take her place on the reviewing stand in front of the Public Library, where Mayor Mitchel, city officials and other dignitaries with their wives were standing.[11]

Despite all the organisation and all the work for the campaign the amendment was defeated. Women had to wait another five years before they could exercise their vote, but out of the campaign had come the closeness of a sisterhood and a knowledge that women could organise themselves to fight against what was an injustice. It is not surprising, considering Jane Mander's background, and her concern for fair play and the rights of the individual, that she was involved so closely with the 1915 campaign.

Jane's interest in reform was not confined to the suffrage issue. She had become very interested in prison reform. Somehow she had become involved with working on a research project for the Church Forum of the Church of the Messiah in New York City. It seems out of character that Jane should suddenly become a church-goer, as she had long ago spurned any sort of organised religion. However, it may be that it was the church which funded the research. Her task was to look at the early life and training of prisoners incarcerated in Sing Sing Prison who were under twenty-four years of age. She was particularly impressed with the work being done by Thomas Mott Osborne, who was the Warden at that time. Osborne had gained notoriety as a prison reformer at Auburn, when he lived among the prisoners to learn about prison life. He was a vocal and harsh critic of the Auburn prison system. At Auburn he established the first democratic organisation of prisoners, the Mutual Welfare League. His work at Auburn brought him to the attention of the governor and superintendent at Sing Sing, and in 1914 he was asked to become Warden there, where he helped to establish a second Mutual Welfare League.[12] Many of the reforms Osborne initially made were simple and were aimed at giving the inmates a sense of worth and dignity. For example, he allowed the prisoners to have visitors on Sunday, something which previously had never been allowed, even though it was a day when it was more likely that families would be able to visit the prisoner. The inmates were allowed to purchase postage stamps and write necessary letters to persons not on the official correspondence list. Lights were left on for half an hour each night, so that inmates could read. Films were moved from Saturday afternoon to Sunday afternoon, providing an interlude on that worst day.[13]

Osborne's success and popularity was borne out when after a fortnight's holiday he was feted on his return by the prisoners:

> Near the prison itself the procession was stopped momentarily when one of the trusties with outside privileges rushed to the Warden's car and thrust a large bouquet of roses into his hand. Flags and bunting decorated the front of the prison itself and were festooned over the doorway. As the Warden stepped into the prison he was confronted with a huge placard which read 'Welcome Home'.[14]

This was the mission which Jane found herself a part of. To Tommy she writes:

> *I forget if I told you about my prisoner in Sing Sing – who has written me two letters a week for five months. He is a most unusual person. He has people working now to get him out, for it's ridiculous keeping him there any longer. The laws of this state are appalling. He has some fine friends, and deserves them. When I got back here I found waiting for me a beautiful black and gold pearl brooch that he had bought in the Prison Store, and sent to greet me on my return to the city. Wasn't that nice? He has some money – there are many very wealthy prisoners in Sing Sing. It is certainly a most remarkable place. I go to spend the day in it on Saturday. Mr Osborne, who had spent a fortnight's holiday away, returned yesterday, and the papers this morning are full of the wonderful reception the prisoners gave him. He is the most amazing being I ever expect to know. If I were only ten years younger I would certainly turn manhunter for all I was worth – only it wouldn't get him. He is a widower, and a multi-millionaire, and gloriously good-looking. He is fifty-five with the saddest face I ever saw.*[15]

Sadly Thomas Mott Osborne was ousted from his position, by what the *New Republic* described as 'The old prison ring, the crowd whose graft has been stopped'. Stories in newspapers started to appear, giving the impression that 'under Mr Osborne Sing Sing is a pleasure resort, a place of turmoil, of friction and anarchy'.[16]

No more is heard of Jane's work at Sing Sing, but it underscores her concern for humanity, and her hatred of injustice. What was to be of greater importance, though, was her need to be involved with work to help alleviate suffering caused by the war.

CHAPTER EIGHT

≈

The old life is like a dream sometimes.
It seems so quiet and remote.
Letter to Tommy, Jane's sister

The year 1915 came to an end and Jane opted out of college. She had been ill, suffering from overwork and tiredness while trying to survive on her small income in such a voracious city. She was writing and having articles accepted. She now felt that it was better to get on with writing and leave behind the difficulties of finding enough money for semester fees. She moved from her rooms at Miss Hill's, which had been close to the college, to a small flat at 117 Waverly Place, off Washington Square. She shared the space with another friend, Ethel Rankin. They had the top floor, Ethel occupying the front rooms and Jane the back. There were three entrance doors and the two areas were divided by a hall. The bathroom they shared. It was much cheaper than the room Jane had in Morningside Drive, in fact she was paying less for three rooms and a bathroom than she had paid for one room at Janus Court. Ethel's windows looked out on to Washington Square, one of the little parks that dot Manhattan; although Jane didn't have a view from her room, she could go out onto the roof and look across the city. It was cheap because there was no elevator, and they had to climb four floors. Also there was gas but no electricity. Jane's own feelings about the move into a place of her own are mirrored in *The Besieging City*, when her heroine Christine Mayne moves into a flat in Waverly Place:

> For three years now Chris had lived in a university rooming house crowded with people she knew well enough to talk to whenever she wanted company. She had, in fact, become very tired of feeling the crowded vibrations of a host of people always about her. For some time she had longed for a place of her own in a house where she knew no one. She had an extra-ordinary sense of peace as she stood this first night by herself in the only place she had so far in her life been able to call her own.[1]

In a talk given to the YWCA in Auckland in 1932, Jane describes a flat similar to the one she lived in at Waverly Place:

The one room means a large bed-sitting room with three doors at one side or end. These lead into a kitchenette, a bathroom, and a huge clothes and trunk cupboard. The kitchenettes are marvels of what can be done in a small space. You stand in the middle of them and reach everything. A combination cabinet holds your china, your food jars, and tins, your vegetables, your groceries. A refrigerator which makes your ice holds your perishable food. A little lift with electric bells brings up your parcels from the basement. A chute opens its mouth and swallows up all your rubbish and conveys it down below. An electric cooker makes no dirt. The window ledge will be plate glass, the kitchen sink porcelain. You hardly need take a step in this place. Then outside your front door is the letter chute that runs your mail down to a central box below. The bathrooms, of course, are famous, small in these tiny flats, but glittering with tiles, glass and porcelain, and warmed with hot water pipes. The living room may be anything its owner likes to make it ....The divan bed is now the thing. With its gay cover and cushions it is a lounge, and the old fear of letting a man see a bed has I suppose gone too. At any rate in these one-roomed modern flats there is no suggestion of bedroom, nor need any male caller know you haven't got one. The room is a library, dining room, living room, and all sorts of combination pieces of furniture have been designed for use in it to save space and serve double purposes.[2]

Jane's need for privacy, for a place for herself with no interruptions, had become more important to her. She was long past the need to be surrounded by the crowds at Whittier Hall. With Ethel just down the hall she would not be lonely, but they could still lead their own individual lives. She could never quite accepted the frenzy of New York, and a retreat which was quiet and her own meant she could work harder on her book. She created an environment for herself which was calm and attractive, something which would be a sanctuary after the hectic atmosphere of Manhattan. In the concrete towers of New York, Jane missed the bush, the creeks and the hills of New Zealand. Having no garden with flowers was another lack she felt, and flowers were too expensive for her to buy. Once she suffered what she called a minor tragedy when a pot of scarlet verbena which she had paid a lot of money for fell off the window ledge and smashed on the court several storeys down. At that time she couldn't afford to buy another.

Her new home was in Greenwich Village, the centre of New York's bohemian life. In the house across the road, Edgar Allen Poe had read his poems from *The Raven*.

As well as being in what was New York's centre for artists, Jane was now also close to the home of the Washington Square Players. She had become very involved with amateur theatre, as a supporter rather than as an actor or director, and she applauded the rise of the small theatre groups. The Washington Square Players remained purely amateur, and its philosophy was to produce only one-act plays. However, eventually it ran out of one-act plays and some of the more adventurous members decided to start a larger subscription theatre, and so later in 1919 the Theatre Guild of New York was born. Jane was one of the foundation members. In a radio manuscript entitled 'Little Theatre Movement in New York and England' Jane writes:

> A new place was found, and a foreign play *Lilliom* was chosen to begin with, with young Joseph Shilkraut and Eva Le Galienne in the leading parts. It proved a surprising success, and then it produced *John Ferguson* a little-known play by Mr St. John Irvine, the well-known drama critic of the London *Observer*. To the astonishment of everybody this grim play ran for nine months and the Guild was launched. ... It combed Europe for interesting foreign plays all novelties to the New York public then. It began on George Bernard Shaw, and gave an even finer performance of *Heartbreak House* than I saw recently in London. By this time, of course, it was paying salaries. Then it further astonished everybody by producing *Back to Methuselah* Mr Shaw's longest work, in a cycle. Instead of losing heavily as they expected they came out about even. The hard heart of Mr Bernard Shaw was so moved that he gave the Theatre Guild the sole rights in America of all his plays, and wrote to the company that if anything could take him to so barbarous a place in New York their work would.[3]

Jane also became involved with another amateur group in Greenwich Village which was started up to assist local playwrights. As she says, 'Nobody could have foreseen the excitement to be raised later by the plays of the now famous O'Neill, who for years was produced solely by this little group.'

Their greatest coup was the premier of O'Neill's best play *The Emperor Jones*. The Negro lead was an actor in the Harlem Negro Theatre, who had been running on elevator before he was chosen for the part. Jane describes the first night:

> I went on the opening night, and I don't think I have ever known a more exciting night in any theatre, or ever seen a more magnificent performance than John Gilpin gave. He was simply inspired, and remained so for the months he played the part, and though Paul Robeson gave a fine performance later on in London he was not John Gilpin. Then, to make the play even more thrilling, we had the wonderful Japanese dancer, Michio Itow, then not well-known, and out of work, to do the witch doctor's dance, and when he appeared in the forest scene the hair of everybody stood on end. To heighten the effect jungle tom-toms were beaten behind the stage from the time the doors opened to the time that the audience regretfully filed out. Recruits had to be brought in to do this continuous beating for over three hours. The device was marvellously successful. The play took the city by storm. The uptown managers raced down, but could not buy it away from the company who moved it to a larger theatre where it ran for months. This performance brought the leading critics down to the barn-like theatre always afterwards, and put the players on

the map, and up to the time that I came away they continued their winter seasons, producing plays for two weeks at a time.[4]

Jane had again made one of her major shifts; this time the distance was not so great as from New Zealand to New York, but she was now no longer a part of the academic world of Barnard, and one would think, far removed from the land of ferns and kauri. However, it was the kauri which was foremost in her mind, because at this stage she was writing *The Story of a New Zealand River*. She had been greatly influenced by Olive Schreiner's book *The Story of an African Farm* and she continually recommended it to her friends to read. Jane was absolutely determined to have her own novel published and continued working on it throughout 1916. In the same year, she had two articles published in the *New Republic*. The first 'A Diary of Evolution' was almost a diary of events in her own life.

In a Small Country Town

Age	
5-12	Accept Bible as written, God, Christ, and The Angels in toto, Fixed Heaven and Hell, the Good and the Bad.
12-14	Believe Bible 'inspired' but not all 'literal'. Shed Fixed Hell. See Satan as a Force of Evil. Doubt Divinity of Christ.
14-16	Read Bible as history and legend. Shed Divinity of Christ, and The Angels. Keep God as Love, Justice and Father of Mankind. Have fixed ideas of Right and Wrong, but become interested in the Bad.
16-18	Browning stage. Frame 'God's in His Heaven, All's Right With the World'. Parade aggressive Optimism. Accept 'World as it is'. Preach Duty of Cheerfulness etc. Orthodox as to Poverty and the Working Classes.
18-19	Honest Doubt. Learn Omar Khayyam by heart. Shed Heaven. Question Personal God. Put away 'God's in His Heaven'. More liberal as to Sin.
19-22	General mental tangle. Study Theosophy and Reincarnation, Spiritualism and Christian Science. Shed Personal God. Call Him Force, the First Cause, the Guiding Principle, Universal Law, etc. Believe in Mind Over Matter, and Love as Constructive Force. Shed fixed ideas of Right and Wrong. See Sin as Defective Education. Morality the new religion. Frame Henley's 'Invictus'. Exalt the Self. Believe in Human Nature. Get first glimmer of Evolution. Hear vaguely of Socialism. Realize the Brotherhood of Man with due regard for Classes and Types.

In New York

22-23	Discover Bernard Shaw. Shed everything else.
23-25	Plunge into psychology, biology, history. Doubt everything but Scientific Facts. Shed God in any form. Learn the Relativity of Truth.

≈ TOP: WHANGAREI TENNIS CLUB, C. 1910. JANE MANDER IS FOURTH FROM RIGHT, MIDDLE ROW. NORTHERN ADVOCATE

≈ BOTTOM: WHANGAREI GOLF CLUB, C. 1910. JANET MANDER (JANE'S MOTHER), CENTRE, SECOND ROW; FRANK MANDER (JANE'S FATHER), SECOND FROM LEFT, BACK ROW; ANNE MANDER, THIRD FROM RIGHT, BACK ROW. COURTESY OF JUDY BEETHAM

≈ JANE MANDER, DRESSED READY TO LEAVE HOME, ON THE STEPS OF THE
HOUSE AT HATEA DRIVE, C. 1910. WHANGAREI MUSEUM

≈ Janet Mander, c. 1912. A rare photograph of Jane's mother, opening the Whangarei to Onerahi railway line. Frank Mander assists. Northern Advocate

≈ THE HOME OF SUSANNAH CLAYTON AT STEWARTS BAY, ON THE KAIWAKA RIVER, 1971. THIS PROVIDED THE MODEL FOR MRS BRAYTON'S HOUSE IN *THE STORY OF A NEW ZEALAND RIVER*. COURTESY OF ALWYN O'CONNOR

Meet Socialists. Investigate Sex War and Wage War. Have Temperament. Exalt the Intellect. Despise the Average Person. Put 'Invictus' away in a drawer.

25-26   Begin again. The new religion – socialism; the new god – humanity; the new Christ – the man, the carpenter; the new devils – poverty, capitalism; the new heaven and hell – the earth; the new Bible – Marx Wells, The Fabian Society, The Economists; the new sins – ignorance, indifference; the new temples – the street corner, the lecture hall; the new idealism – liberté, égalité, fraternité; the new words – Individualism, Communism, Humanitarianism.

26-28   Preach Radicalism, Anarchism, Agitation, and No Compromise. Despise Laws, Ceremonies, Traditions, and Precedents. Believe in Free Love. Exalt sincerity. Proclaim The Facts of Life. Lose temperament in the flurry of general destruction. Tolerate all Comrades in the March of Progress. Believe in The People and the Natural Rights of Man.

28-30   Doubt adequacy of Anarchism. Begin to suspect The People. Consider Organization, Co-operation, and Education. Study Unions and Statistics. See need for Some Compromise. Shed Anarchism and Agitation.

30-32   Join a union. Believe in the Wage War. Preach Unity and Sacrifice for the Good of All. Lead Strikes.

32-33   Doubt possibility of Unity. Suspect motives of leaders. Question effectiveness of Sacrifice. Hazy as to definition of The Good of All. Lose illusions about The People. See hope in Political Action. Shed Unions and The Working Man.

33-34   Go into politics. Learn the value of Compromise. Suspect the wisdom of Sincerity. Drop Free Love. Uphold Laws and Ceremonies. Hide The Facts of Life. Try Merit and Reason upon the Politician. Suspect the power of Merit and Reason. Try Money and Influence upon the politician. Perceive their immediate and decisive effect. Suspect possibility of Democracy as defined by Lincoln. Suspect the politician. Suspect myself. Begin to feel tired.

34-35   Shed politics and the politicians. Turn to Social Service. Join four Clubs and three Movements. Boost the Feminists and Suffragists. Talk, and listen to talk. Begin to suspect Movements. Suspect all Human Nature. Get more tired.

35-36   A great weariness. Sick of Action. Sick of Words. Sick of Humanity. No illusions left. Shed everything. Do nothing. Turn to Art.

36-37   Believe in Art. Recover Temperament, but don't mention it. Fall in love with an artist. Believe in love. Believe in the artist. Get married.

37   Have a child who will begin it all over again.

This piece mirrors much of Jane's own development, and much of the philosophy was incorporated into the character of Asia in *The Story of a New Zealand River*. In a letter to John A. Lee in 1936 Jane says:

> *I have always been on the side of the young, the new idea, and the under-dog, though perhaps I have not done very much about it. Being (or trying to be) an artist I have never been interested in politics or politicians. I am told I am wrong there. But the world of beauty is my province, and I have never been able to discover much of it in the world of politicians.*[5]

This statement seems odd, since she embraced socialism so wholeheartedly when she was in Sydney. Her articles for *The Maoriland Worker* seem to be forgotten, and if she was not interested in politics, why did she work so hard for the Suffragist Movement in New York? Maybe these actions were nothing to do with the politics of the time. Perhaps socialism was merely the wrapping for feelings Jane had always had for those less fortunate. It did give her an opportunity to write articles pointing out the disparities between the rich and the poor. Maybe as she had so honestly spelled out to her sister, speaking on street corners and being involved with a woman as prestigious as Carrie Chapman-Catt were simply good ways to get herself known.

The second essay, printed in the *New Republic* in June, had a greater impact on the readers and elicited a huge response. Letters relating to it were still being printed in the 2 September edition. The piece, entitled 'Sheltered Daughters', has one of the most telling and self revealing paragraphs which relates to Jane's own struggle to move away from being a 'Sheltered Daughter':

> It is a terrible thing to have to wound the people one loves. Those of us who have gone through it in the fight for personal freedom never quite get over it. Those of us who have turned in the road to look back at the motionless figures in the doorway who have made us feel like murderers when we wanted them to bid us Godspeed as joyous adventurers, who have chilled our enthusiasms so that we feel that we can never turn to them save in pity and tolerance, know that life holds few things sadder. If in the end we can forget the hurts, if we can recover some mutual respect, we have something to be thankful for.

Leaving home had an enormous impact on Jane, determined as she was to make her own way. Her feelings for her family were strong, and her isolation in a city as engulfing as New York would often give her a feeling of separation and distance that was hard to accept. She recreates the experience of leaving home without a blessing when in *The Story of a New Zealand River* Asia leaves:

> As Bruce hauled up the mainsail, Asia sat down by the rudder; then she turned homewards, and seeing the figure in the doorway, scrambled to her feet, and waved.

For the life of her Alice could not wave back. She tried to, but her frozen limbs refused to move. Her throat burned. Her eyes burned. She dimly saw the group on the beach wave with an energy that seemed purposeful to hide her own immobility. She saw the figure in the stern of the boat sit down...

David Bruce did not look at Asia till they were well out into the channel. Then he sat down in the stern beside her, his right hand on the mainsail rope, and his left along the back of the seat behind her as she steered.

He said nothing, knowing she was beyond speech. Once or twice she looked back to see the children still waving from the cliffs, but not the figure at the window.

Presently he saw that tears were dripping off her cheeks.

'She might have waved,' she choked, giving way suddenly.[6]

Jane's own feelings of alienation and of being the outsider provide an inherent quality in most of the heroines in her stories. Her struggle to unshackle the fetters of family so that she could pursue a literary career had come with a price, a price which she recognised even though she had written to Tommy in 1912 not to worry about 'any damned thing and you'll get on just as well'.[7] Despite her insistence on separation from her family, she often mourned her isolation: 'Was so glad to hear what a lovely time you were having camping at Paihia. My! didn't I envy you! Much as I love New York I do long at times for tents and a New Zealand bay'.[8]

For anyone, a fortieth birthday is often a time of taking stock. In 1917 on her birthday Jane was vain enough to be pleased that she looked younger than when she left New Zealand five years before. She had become influenced by the women she knew in America to have her hair shampooed weekly and reported that the girl who did it had 'restored all its life and done wonders to it'. She also now used a good face cream, and was in the habit of drinking lots of cold water everyday; consequently her skin had improved. She had also learned to dress better. 'Americans judge you almost entirely by your clothes. I don't quite agree with it but in New York you'd never get a job or keep it if you didn't dress well'. She was probably happier than she had been for a long time, as she was now a part of a literary and intellectual world, and she was meeting people who were interesting and stimulating. Although she had little money she had learnt how to survive, and to enjoy herself. She also had friends who were kind to her, and her life was approaching something resembling her hopes when she started out for the big city.

Although Jane still received a small allowance from her father, lack of money was always a problem. She managed to acquire a job working for the National Guard Relief for the State, which paid the equivalent of eight pounds per week. Out of her salary she had to pay her rent, as well as buy food and clothing. She calculated that even eating plainly, food would still cost her three pounds per week. But her flat was close to her office, and she could walk to work, and save a bus fare. Her hope to save some money for a trip back to New Zealand faded, as all she earned was taken up with the necessity of survival.

The job she had taken on was to look after the wives and families of the National Guard, a volunteer army used mainly for guard work, riots, and patrolling the Mexican border. Initially there was little to do, for although the States had declared war on Germany Jane reported there was little excitement:

> *It is going to take the States months to get men ready – and we don't expect much trouble. Spies are being hunted down everywhere. The chief trouble in America in times of excitement is from cranks and lunatics, of whom thousands are wandering around and anything unusual drives them batty.*[10]

Although the job was not well paid, it did bring forth some other benefits. It was through it that she became involved with working on the presidential committee for Charles E. Hughes, who was running as the Republican candidate when Woodrow Wilson was running for the post of President. Although Charles E. Hughes was unsuccessful, it was another entrée for Jane into a world of interesting people; it was while she was working on this committee that she met President Roosevelt.

Jane found that the work she was doing was not stimulating enough for her and the salary was low. When the opportunity came for her to work for the Red Cross on Fifth Avenue for a slightly increased wage, she took the job. Not only did it mean she had more money, but it also gave her a feeling of doing something of real importance for the war effort.

Other possible reasons that drove Jane to work for the Red Cross are revealed in a passage from *The Besieging City*. Here she described the feelings Chris Mayne had about working for the Red Cross:

Something half expressed inside her had driven her into that work and in it she now meant to stay as long as the war lasted. But she had moments of hoping to get out of it something more than the satisfaction of 'doing her bit' and enough money to pay for rent and food. She hoped to find in an organisation that had gathered all types of men and women under its banner somebody she could care greatly about.

At first she could think of nothing but adapting herself as quickly as possible to fierce pressure and everlasting noise. The office of the New York County Chapter was in an old house that has long since gone the way of many old houses, on the corner of Thirty-Sixth and Fifth. Chris was near the front of the second floor. She often thought she might just as well have been in the middle of the street. For a month or two she went home at night noise-shocked as she felt men were being shocked in the trenches. At the end of each week she would say to herself she could not stand it for another. But although her appearance brought many predictions of her breakdown she was exceedingly tough.[11]

Chris Mayne was looking for someone about whom she could care. It is rare to get an insight into Jane's intimate life, but it is clear that this was a yearning she had too. Yet she shied away from close relationships with the opposite sex. Friendship was one thing that could be regulated, she could continue to write at her own pace without being distracted by domestic responsibilities. In a letter written in 1913 to her sister, Jane mentions the Davis family trying to match her with one of their apparently handsome cousins, but she remained uninterested in him and was amused by their efforts. In *The Besieging City* Chris Mayne has an affair with the handsome relative, but there are no indications that this was something that happened to Jane. Whatever parallels can be drawn between Jane's life in New York – and there are many – *The Besieging City* is a work of fiction.

It may be, too, that she had a reason for distaste for marriage. She once told Olive de Malmanche that when she and her sister Annie were young they could hear their father importuning her mother to make love. It distressed them so much that they would cover their heads with pillows.[12] Amy, Jane's youngest sister, was the only one of the girls to marry and have children. Annie did not marry until she was in her late middle age, and neither Carrie nor Jane ever married. In *The Story of a New Zealand River,* Asia in a conversation with Mrs Brayton, says:

> Why don't our parents realise that we children have eyes to see and ears to hear? I slept for years with only a thin wall between my parents and me. Slept, did I say? I sat up for hours shivering, sick and faint. I cried, I prayed, I raged. I grew old listening to them. I grew to have a pity and then a contempt for them both, and then just a tolerance. I couldn't understand, and I don't understand now how human beings can be so stupid, and so cruel, and make so much unhappiness for each other.[13]

What Jane had seen of marriage as a child and a young woman had not encouraged her to seek a partner. Marriage also meant children and that would interfere with being a writer, though later she was impressed when she met women writers in London who had families and wrote as well.

There have been suggestions that she may have been a lesbian, but that suggestion probably had more to do with the fact that she returned to New Zealand with a short severe haircut, and wore clothes that were devoid of flounces. Her style of dress suited her tall thin frame – it was smart – influenced by living in New York, and her loud dogmatic voice made her appear eccentric. Putting all these things together and that fact that she never married, some people have made the assumption she was lesbian. She was friendly with many people, male and female. She lived with other women at various times, but that was probably more for economic reasons than romantic, and sharing accommodation with a man you were not married to in the 1920s was generally not acceptable. Jane was a person who maintained her private life as just that – private. A great burner of letters, she destroyed many letters she received and nothing has come to light that suggests that she had a lover, whether male or female.

What Jane did have, however, was a great organising ability. This meant that before long she was in charge of the financial side of all the Red Cross workrooms on Manhattan Island. There were 560 of them. An enormous cross-section of people worked in them, from women who belonged to the Daughters of the Revolution to waitresses from the lower east side. Some of New York's most notable citizens allowed their homes to be used as workrooms: Ann Morgan who was the daughter of Pierpont Morgan, Mrs Willy K. Vanderbilt and John D. Rockefeller. Jane would often talk with John D. Rockefeller and described him as looking like a little wizened mummy. She remained unimpressed with his house however, and thought it was gloomy inside with too much carved mahogany.

As well as workrooms in private houses there were rooms in some of the big clubs such as the Colony Club, and all these came under Jane's jurisdiction. Once again Jane's heroine in *The Besieging City* recreates what she herself felt and thought when she worked for the Red Cross:

> It was not till it was all over that Chris realised how thoroughly Manhattan Island, which was the special province of her office, had been nutshelled under that one roof. Every grade of wealth and poverty was represented there: from the rich women of the Colony Club to the factory girls of the poorest social centre. Every quarter of the city had its workrooms, from the borders of the Harlem Canal to the Bowling Green, and from the West Side docks to Avenue A. Every organisation, racial, religious, educational, artistic, industrial, and diversional. Every kind of house from the palaces of the Vanderbilts and Rockefellers, from the gymnasiums and roofs of great clubs down to the vestry of a little slum mission hall. Some five hundred and fifty circles, all revolving about their individual master spirits.[14]

Amazingly, considering how hard she had been working, Jane finished *The Story of a New Zealand River* by the beginning of 1917 but because of her enormous workload with the Red Cross she put it to one side.

Later in that year she had a lucky meeting with a friend of John Lane's American manager. The friend persuaded her to let him pass the manuscript on to John Lane in America. The American editors liked the book and sent it to London with a strong recommendation for publication. For a long time nothing was heard. As Jane said 'There was then one of those colossal silences that daunt the stoutest writer.'[15]

One night in 1918 she arrived home exhausted after a long difficult day at the Red Cross, to find a letter from Mr Lane himself saying that he would publish her book if she agreed to a couple of cuts. Years later at a dinner of the PEN club in London, Mr Edward Garnett told her that he had read the book in typescript and had recommended it to John Lane. It was the only novel by an unknown writer taken on by the firm in 1918.

At the end of 1918 Jane was involved with the largest debarkation hospital. In fact she spent Christmas Day working with 4500 men who had returned from the trenches. There were concerts on every floor of the hospital, as well as Christmas Dinner. Women from the Red Cross had made 15,000 stockings for four of the hospitals. Jane described it as a city of sick and wounded and convalescent men, but with cheerfulness and smiles everywhere.

> *I was rejoiced to hear the American boys say everywhere they like the Australian and New Zealanders for friends best of all the troops, and that was before they knew I was a New Zealander. One boy showed me with pride a belt with Australian and New Zealand trophies, and Australian and New Zealand coins, and told me the stories of the men who had worn them.*[16]

Jane's most joyful news for 1918 though, was to tell her mother that her book had been accepted and that it would be published in the (Northern) spring of 1919. 'I shan't make any money out of it for some months, but I now have prospects'.

CHAPTER NINE

≈

*I am going to lots of fine music this winter
as I shall not be here next.*
Letter to Tommy, 30 December 1918

In 1919 Jane continued working with the Red Cross until June, as she had promised. She was earning the equivalent of nine pounds a week; by being very frugal she was able to save half of what she was earning. Already in her mind was the possibility of leaving America and going to London. She had also been offered two other jobs after she finished with the Red Cross; even if she didn't make a lot of money from *The Story of a New Zealand River*, she would still have something to live on.

The novel was published in New York in 1920. Its publication had been delayed by the war years, due to the shortage of labour and the increased cost of materials. When finally it was published the occasion was almost an anticlimax for Jane, it had taken such a long time for her first book to become a reality: 'From my childhood days I had dreamed of the day when my first book would be published, but when it came to my flat in New York I was too tired even to open the parcel'.[1]

However, she was happy with the reviews in the U.S.A. and in Australia and New Zealand. In America good reviews appeared in the *Washington Star*, *San Francisco Argonaut*, *Indianapolis News*, *New York Times*, *New York Tribune*, and *The Dispatcher* in Pittsburgh. Most reviews commented on her fresh style, although some reviewers thought the book was too long and that it could have been shortened. The *New York Times* said it was 'clever but overlong'. *The Times* reviewer in London said:

> The authoress has a real ability to describe character and differences of outlook, but she does not allow the plot to become lost in disquisitions. The book would have been more emphatic if it could be shortened but in its present form it is a patient study of one example of the immemorial clash between impulse and convention. The authoress never exactly hits the bullseye, but she's always on target.

The *Sydney Mail* said it was 'The best novel that has yet come from our neighbouring dominion'. Only the *Evening Post* refers to it as the a novel which 'comes under the category of sex-problem fiction.' Elsewhere reviewers regarded the book as one with strong characterisation, and most agreed with the *New Zealand Herald,* which said:

> What matters most – whether or not one accepts Miss Mander's challenge – is that this is a real novel, written of a real New Zealand which can enter the lists of any large reading town of the world. The technical side of it is good.

Whangarei readers, though, were not considering the technicalities of the writing. Many people felt they had been portrayed in the book in uncomplimentary ways. Some recognised themselves or thought they recognised themselves and an uproar ensued. Apart from the people who were unhappy at feeling they had been included in the book, there were those who thought Jane was condoning extra-marital relationships, and that the book contained too much sex. Much to Jane's amusement, the book was placed on the discretionary shelf at the Whangarei Public Library. This meant that those who wished to read the novel had to apply to the librarian, who would then decide if that person was a fit reader. What criteria the librarian used in decision-making has not been explored but apparently the story was considered far too racy for the readers of Whangarei. Elsewhere though the book was well received. Eventually the clamour to read the book in Whangarei overtook the initial prudery, and soon the one copy the library had looked very worn.

Sales of *The Story of a New Zealand River* were not large and did not make Jane a wealthy woman; she continued to write articles and contribute to magazines and periodicals, as well as work part-time in order to support herself financially. Pleased as she was with the reception of her book, it would never have crossed her mind that her first novel would enjoy such durability, and that it would continue to be republished at intervals over a period of seventy years.

Following on from the success of *The Story of a New Zealand River* was the need to get down to writing the second novel, often the stumbling block for an author who has first novel success. As she said later in a letter to John A. Lee, 'second books are the snag on which so many writers founder. I did myself so I know.'[2]

At a dinner party with friends in New York, Jane met Ralph Block who was a scenario reader for the Goldwyn Company in New York. Films were the coming thing, and writing for films was where Jane could make money and a name for herself. He persuaded her to write her next stories with an eye to their being made into films. As a result her next two books, *The Passionate Puritan* and *The Strange Attraction,* were written with this idea in mind. Jane later regarded this as a very misguided venture, 'a mistake I ever afterwards regretted'.[3] She said the novels were shallow because they were written for a medium which demanded no depth. 'How I ever came to fall for the idea of writing for films I do not know. But at the time so many better writers than I were trying to do the same thing – but what a waste of my time – and I never could recover later on, what with the time and energy I had to give to earning my living by manuscript reading'.[4] In a letter to John A. Lee she reiterates her contempt for the movies: 'Oh my god, John Lee, how are we going to save the souls and minds of people in this land from the pernicious bunk of the American movies.'[5] Neither novel had the sparkle and power or freshness of *The Story of a New Zealand River*.

The Passionate Puritan, which Jane had dedicated to her brother, is the story of a young school teacher, Sidney Carey, going to the backblocks of the north to teach at a small country school. The setting and school are similar to the places in which Jane taught when she was a young school teacher. The book had some reasonable reviews. The Sunday Observer (an undated clipping) says of it, 'It is delightful to find a sex-problem dealt with sanely, honestly and incidents such as a great fire made alive without heroics or sentimentality.' But the *New Zealand Herald* says:

> The local colour and the general background of the story is really good. The actual plot – perhaps we are all tiring of sex problems in our fiction ... the dialogue is thin often trivial in characters.

Another critic was Alan Mulgan, who believed Jane was too obsessed with sex in her stories:

> Miss Mander's chief fault is her obsession with sex; a little more reticence would do her no harm. Her second book *The Passionate Puritan* is so inferior to her first that one looks forward to her third with a little anxiety.[6]

The book isn't as bad as Mulgan appears to think, for once again Jane tackles the theme of independence for women, the right to have a career and to be in charge of one's own destiny. As to her obsession with sex, she was trying to portray people as they really were and not gloss over the importance sex has in every person's life. Of course, this made her very 'modern' for her time.

Jane's third novel, *The Strange Attraction*, drew on her experiences when working on a newspaper in Dargaville. The portion of the story which deals with the election is reminiscent of the time when her father was standing for the Reform Party. In this novel she goes further in looking at freedom and independence for women; her heroine enters into a secret marriage with a man who is a drug addict. Although they are married, it appears to outsiders that the couple are living 'in sin'.

Again she had reasonable reviews. *The Literary Digest International Book*

Review in January 1923 says that 'Miss Mander has proved in this novel that she is a skilled literary artist in dialog[sic] plot, construction, style characterization.' According to the *Times Literary Supplement* reviewer, ' This well-told story is a thoroughly competent piece of work, with an adequate plot, real atmosphere, and considerable psychological interest.' But the *Daily News* takes a different perspective: 'If Miss Mander could forget Freedom, Independence, Sex and Equality, she might write a good novel.'

More critics joined the bandwagon, accusing her of being 'sex obsessed', until finally she could no longer remain silent. In the *Auckland Star* in February 1924, her rebuttal of her New Zealand critics was printed under the headline 'Miss Jane Mander's Novels – the Author's Reply to Critics':

> Dear Sir — As you were interested enough to publish the most impersonal review I have yet seen from the New Zealand Press of my third novel, and one that gave unusually representative quotations, I ask space to reply through your columns to some of the remarks of my New Zealand critics.
>
> I really cannot understand why some of them call me sex-obsessed. Am I being compared out there with the publications of the Religious Tract Society? If I am being compared, as I should be with the modern novel writers on this side of the world, that term cannot truthfully be applied to me. As a matter of fact I'm not half sexy enough for hundreds of thousands of readers here. The people who read my books here read them for the New Zealand colour and certainly not for the sex-element. I can think of only one review I have seen in the Old World that used the term in connection with my work. Some of my New Zealand critics must be ignorant of the work of D.H. Lawrence, Dorothy Richardson, May Sinclair, Aldous Huxley (England), Sherwood Anderson, Ben Hecht, Floyd Dell (American), Wassermann (Austria), Papini and Borghese (Italy) and of Paul Morand, Jean Cocteau, Jean Giradeau [sic] (France), to mention only a few, all people whose work has been boosted and admired by the leading critics. Truly these people are far greater artists than I, but my books are Sunday School tracts in comparison with the sophisticated stuff they are doing.
>
> I suspect some of my New Zealand critics of motives of policy in dealing with an isolated and perhaps provincial average person. But I am not going to make the mistake of thinking that intelligent adults have ceased to exist in New Zealand, and my books are written for intelligent adults. I am going to keep on believing that my native land is producing about the same number of intelligent adults per thousand of population as any other British country. It is unfortunate that the general newspaper has to be run for the average person, but at least the average person need not be misinformed.
>
> I have been accused of putting into my third book characters who are 'unrepresentative' of the community in which they are placed. Now a writer

who is trying to be an artist, as I sincerely am has nothing whatever to do with being a tourist agent, or a photographer, or a historian, or a compiler of community statistics. The question for critics is not did two such people as Valerie Carr and Dane Barrington ever actually live in Dargaville, but might they have lived there? And the answer is that exceptional people may be found anywhere. And even if it has to be a question of fact anyone who ever lived in the North of New Zealand for many years, as I did must have been struck over and over again by finding the most unlikely people in out-of-the way places. If there was one thing significant about our North it was just that. I could not begin to put into books all the 'unrepresentative' people we came across in the bushes about the gumfields, and in the small towns. But why should they not be written about? As a matter of fact it is just such people who interest many a novelist. In my first novel I put an old English lady into the wilds. She was entirely 'unrepresentative' of the community in which she was placed, but I have not seen any objection to her on that score.

Critics need not be afraid that my readers on this side of the world will think Valerie Carr a typical New Zealander. It must be obvious to anybody of the most ordinary intelligence that Valerie and Dane are exceptional people and not typical of anything. The question for critics again is did I make my exceptional people credible? And that is exactly what the critics here think I did do.

Now critics are well within their rights in saying they do not like my people. That is a personal opinion that many critics now give in otherwise dispassionate judgement. Many writers today are writing fine books about boring or disagreeable people. In spite of much opinion to the contrary, I detested Johanna Godden in Sheila Kay Smith's great novel of that name, but my dislike of the character is something apart from my judgement of the book, which I regard as the finest work of art in novel form produced by an Englishwoman in many a year. A Novel should be judged like any other work 'by laws deduced from itself; whether or not it be consistent with itself is the question'. In other words, how well does an author do what he sets out to do? A critic who damns a book entirely because he does not like the leading characters has something to learn about criticism. I know well enough that such personal opinion is given in places outside of New Zealand. My compatriots are by no means the only sinners in that respect.

Then I have been accused of 'hitting' at things. I suspect again that sensitiveness explored by modern psychologists and labelled the inferiority complex. But I assure my critics I am not 'hitting' at anything. I am trying to be an artist. Nobody knows better than I that I have a lot to learn, and nobody knows better than I that to be an artist one must not be petty. Simply because I use, as every other writer does, the material of my experience, I have this charge levelled at me. But I take comfort in knowing there is hardly a writer who is not accused of the same crime. It is quite legitimate to use the name of a place. Nobody who reads my books here will suppose that Dargaville is any different from the countless small towns all over the world or that the fashionable suburb of Remuera is any worse than any other fashionable suburb simply because my unconventional character came out of it. Really we writers are not taken as literally as all that.

And furthermore, I am not trying to shock anybody. I am writing to please myself, without any thought as to whether I am pleasing or annoying or shocking anybody else. If an artist stops to consider any section of his public, or what his friends would like, or what his publisher would like, or anything at all but that inner light inside himself, he ceases to be an artist and becomes a purveyor of goods. Unfortunately there are too many purveyors of goods trying to masquerade as artists in the world today. I am simply trying to be honest and to be loyal to my own experience.

Yours truly Jane Mander (London 22 December 1923)

Jane in her self-enforced exile was vulnerable to criticism in her home country. Some of her articles had critical reviews in New York, yet she had not responded with the same vigour as this letter portrays. It is as if she was still trying to prove herself to an audience far removed from where she was now resident:

The exile ... is like a bird forced by chill weather at home to migrate, but always poised to fly back. He is political in that he has suffered the chill of official displeasure in some form or other or at least he feels unwelcome and waits for the weather to change.[7]

Jane was ready to make another transition, not yet to fly home like the godwits, but this time to leave New York behind and go to London. Her publisher John Lane was based in London, and the hectic atmosphere of New York, which had initially been so stimulating, had lost its glow. She had always been surprised at how she stood the noise, which she once described as 'fiendish'. The noise from the overhead railways she thought was 'just awful'. Her second and third books had not been as successful as she had hoped, and she believed it was time to move on. She had been in New York for eleven years. Many of the women she had been friendly with at Barnard were now married and bringing up families; everything had changed, she was tired and needed to have a different atmosphere in which to revitalise herself, so that she could continue with her work. Before she left New York, though, she had the joy of a visit from Annie, her younger sister, who had completed her nursing training in New Zealand and was working for a few months at the Presbyterian Hospital in New York. For Jane it was a marvellous reunion, for it was the only time in twenty years overseas that she saw any member of her family.[8]

CHAPTER TEN

≈

*It is quite a journey from the forests of
the north of New Zealand to
the borders of Chelsea.*
'The Making of an Authoress' by Jane Mander[1]

Arriving back in London in 1923 was for Jane something like a homecoming. The mental horizons were immeasurably wider than they were in either New Zealand or Australia, and Jane thought that even the most cosmopolitan American would have to admit that for personal liberty and for democracy of the mind, London led the world. She wrote,

> London is one of the few places in the world where you may be as eccentric as you choose and go unremarked. ... London allows you to be different, to think what you like, to wear what you like, to come and go as you please without spying upon you. You live your own life. As long as you do not annoy your neighbours by making that life noisy, your neighbours will not annoy you. Whatever your secret thoughts or ambitions you will find people to whom you are not afraid to speak them.[2]

Jane's publisher John Lane and his wife were very kind and took her in as one of their own. Lloyd Morris, a leading critic in New York and a good friend, had given her introductions to relatives of his who lived in London. It was through the Morris relations that Jane met Victor Gollancz, who had just started his own company and was regarded as a brilliant young publisher. Victor had different ideas about publicising books and soon had everybody in the publishing world imitating his type and his advertisements. 'But nobody can imitate the huge parties he has given to most of literary London'.[3] Jane was invited to two of these parties, which were held at Claridges – where the cost of champagne alone would have broken most other publishers. At the first one she attended there was so much noise made by the distinguished literary gathering that an Indian Prince, who had the suite above the banqueting hall, sent two dignified turbaned servants down to request the management to stop the racket. The protest didn't have much effect and the party roared on. Hardly a writer or critic was missing, because Gollancz would always invite authors he thought were interesting to the parties, whether they were his own or not.

Jane had always wanted to meet Rose Macaulay, who was known not only as a writer but as one of the most inveterate party-goers in London, and it was at a Gollancz party that Jane finally met her. But she was disappointed by her appearance. Used to New York women who dressed so well, she couldn't get over her surprise that Rose appeared old-maidish, and dowdy, the last thing she thought one would expect from someone who had such a keen and incisive pen. Jane found her frank and pleasant, but with her New York bias it was an anticlimax for her to discover that someone she had admired could look so unprepossessing.

She had not been in London very long before she was introduced to Rebecca West. The meeting was a Pen Club dinner where there were eighty-seven of London's leading writers. Seated at her table were, amongst others, John Galsworthy and May Sinclair. She also met Edward Garnett, who told her that it was he who had recommended her first novel to John Lane, and she met Radclyffe Hall, H.G. Wells and Arnold Bennett. Jane thought that Radclyffe Hall was one of the few Englishwomen she had met on her return to England who knew how to dress! At last this was the life she had desired, mixing with and being a part of the great London literary scene. It was what she had dreamed of when she sat in her room at the top of the house in Whangarei. It was what she had dreamed of as she had put a paper to bed in Dargaville. It was what she had dreamed of as she went without meals in the frugal life she had imposed on herself in New York.

Delighted as she was to find herself in such dramatic company, Jane soon found that to support herself in London she would have to accept any work that was available. London in post-war days was now expensive. 'The minimum cost for a woman living alone in ordinary decent comfort in one room, could not be less than four pounds a week in any decent neighbourhood.'[4] A boarding house was out of the question in Jane's computations!

She began writing articles and short stories for any magazine or newspaper which would accept her work, and was pleased when one of her articles was accepted by *Time and Tide*, a magazine founded by Viscountess Rhondda in 1920. This magazine was set up as an independent non-party weekly review, a periodical which espoused the suffragist cause and was a place for the woman's voice to be heard. It attracted many clever women writers, including Rebecca West, E.M. Delafield, Cicely Hamilton, Naomi Mitchison and Sylvia Lynd.

Jane's article appeared in 1924 and was entitled 'Flats for Single Women'; it compared accommodation available for working women in

≈ THE LONG HAIR HAS GONE. JANE MANDER'S PASSPORT PHOTOGRAPH, 1914.

≈ Top: Columbia University, New York, 1995.

≈ Bottom: Barnard College, New York, 1995. Jane attended this women's college before she enrolled for the journalism course at Columbia.

≈ In 1915 Jane Mander's home was in the apartment on the top floor of this building, 117 Waverly Place, New York (1995).

≈ LEFT:
PUBLISHED
AUTHOR. JANE
IN NEW YORK
IN 1920, THE
YEAR THAT
*THE STORY OF
A NEW
ZEALAND RIVER*
WAS
PUBLISHED.

≈ RIGHT:
ANOTHER
PORTRAIT,
SOMETIME IN
THE 1920s,
POSSIBLY IN
NEW YORK.
BOTH
AUCKLAND
PUBLIC
LIBRARY

London and New York. Jane's surroundings were always important to her; she couldn't tolerate anything that grated, wrong colours put together, ungainly furniture. She desired always to have a serene and comfortable space around her in which to work and to entertain her friends.

> Coming recently from ten years in New York to London I have been enormously interested by the contrasts in living conditions offered by the two great cities. London is all to the good for one's nerves, and yet strangely inadequate when it comes to conveniences that are ancient history to New Yorkers. And while I love London more every day for its birds, beasts, flowers and many other things, I have a grievance against it that grows hotter with the passage of time. And as I am British I trust I will be allowed to grumble about it. London has not yet recognised the needs and desires of the poorer single woman in the way New York has. It has not begun to give her decent living conditions at a price she can afford to pay. The London landlord has not begun to think about her. And until the landlord has begun to think about you there is much lacking to the peace of your days.[5]

She was particularly scathing of boarding houses, and was appalled that for single women that was about all that was on offer for a reasonable rent. 'I defy anybody to make anything impressive of a boarding house except a funeral pyre.'[6]

As well as writing articles for any periodical which would take her work, she took up the job of Reader for John Lane. It was a job she loathed, she referred to it as 'hack work' and said that she learned first-hand what she had known second-hand: 'that the muck that is finally seen in print is as nothing to the muck that gets written but not published'.[7]

However, although this work was not what Jane wanted to do, it did mean that she met some younger writers and helped them to revise their early books, something that she became very good at. She would later help Monte Holcroft, Mona Tracy and other struggling New Zealand authors. One of the writers she helped at Lane's was Georgette Heyer, who became a good friend.

In 1924 Jane also started writing her column for the Christchurch edition of the *Sun* newspaper. It appeared initially under the banner 'At the Sign of the Fleet'. Then in 1927, when there was an Auckland *Sun*, she wrote for that too. She was introduced in the following way:

> Miss Jane Mander, the New Zealand novelist who was born in North Auckland and has won for herself a distinguished place among British writers is one of *The Sun*'s London correspondents. She will contribute regularly articles on art, literature, and topics of general interest to Aucklanders. Miss Mander has a crisp incisive style of writing and is, above all a fearless critic.[8]

So began a series of articles describing events which Jane thought would be of interest to the people back in New Zealand. People still referred to

England as 'home' and desired above all to hear what was happening in what many then regarded as the centre of the world.

In an article written in 1924, Jane reveals just how little she has received in monetary terms from the sale of her novels:

> The wildest notions exist as to the amount paid to the author in royalties. The standard rate is 10% on the first few thousand copies sold, and on the published price of the same. Ten percent of seven and sixpence is ninepence. Just calculate how many thousands of copies need to be sold before the author makes £50. If a first novel sells 2000 copies in England it is said to have done well. Then on the colonial sale, we writers get threepence a copy. Calculate again how many copies we must sell to our sceptical or admiring compatriots before we make £10 out of those who should be proud to shake us by the hand. Personally, I beg would-be novelists to be dress designers and stenographers and advertising experts, and a dozen other useful things as well. I am supposed to have had a considerable literary success in both England and America. I certainly cannot complain of the amount of publicity I have received, or of the quality of a good many of my reviews. I have written three novels, and I am today hundreds of pounds in debt. That is a confession made in the interests of the optimists.[9]

By this time Jane was living at Cathcart Road in Chelsea, an area which in the 1920s had similarities to Washington Square, where she had lived in New York. It was the patch and seedbed for writers and artists. Her house was a few doors away from John Drinkwater and his wife Daisy Kennedy, and nearby Katherine Mansfield and Middleton Murry had lived. She became friendly with Augustus John and his family, and would often see the sculptor Jacob Epstein. She had found her milieu, at last she was a part of the world of writers and artists – the London world that every wishful colonial artist aspired to. From her articles back to the *Sun* it is easy to see that she is involved in all the exciting events that London could offer.

She went to hear Edith Sitwell read her poems through a megaphone to the 'accompaniment of expressive music'. She admits that she didn't understand the art of Gertrude Stein or Edith Sitwell, but that she was willing to be educated. She referred to the work of Gertrude Stein as being written in some gobbledegook known only to Miss Stein. Whether she was won over to the new-style poetry is debatable, as she concluded her article on the evening out by saying,

> The most interesting thing about the evening was the audience, after all, and the personality of the family [the Sitwells] that could bring them together, for what I suspect was a profitable publicity stunt. For the rest, the lovers of Keats and Tennyson have nothing to fear.[10]

'Come Round London With Me!' is the title of another of her articles and she writes about what is on at the theatres in London. Her knowledge of plays and playwrights is extensive, and she has the added advantage of being able to compare London productions with those of New York, which give her articles balance. Another piece is entitled 'La Vie De Bohème – Nights at the Café Royal'. She loved the atmosphere at the Café, which was the meeting place for writers and artists. It felt French as a casual dropping-in place, and she found the conversation and talk that took place stimulating. Sometimes the Café became over stimulating; she recounts with amusement an incident she witnessed which involved Epstein and one of his models:

> Epstein was dining in the grill [at the Cafe Royal] with one of his models, when three very young men entered and took the table next him. Then began what was obviously some personal attack on their part. They talked in loud voices at Epstein, deriding his work, and particularly the Hyde Park memorial (about which controversy still rages). Epstein stood it with great patience for some time. Then he sprang up and used a wine bottle to some purpose on the body of one of his tormentors. A wineglass was thrown back. But it missed Epstein and hit the lady. By this time the management was on the scene. And the management of the Cafe Royal, I may remark, in passing, is a personage I should not like to be up against. The young men were ordered out and forbidden ever to return. Apologies were made to Epstein, who shortly afterwards withdrew with his model in disgust.[11]

Along with the work of reading manuscripts and writing short stories and articles Jane had started on another novel. It had been in her mind for some time that she would like to write another novel set in the north of New Zealand, but this time from a male perspective. It was a difficult idea and that she managed to pull it off indicates the depth of ability she had gained in her craft.

She had received a letter of encouragement from A.G. Stephens, who was the editor of the Australian literary newspaper *The Bookfellow* in Sydney. He was an author of repute and was regarded as the 'Dean' of Australian letters and the chief critic of art and literature in Australia and New Zealand. The Toronto Public Library once asked him to send 100 books representing Australia and New Zealand literature; and he had included *The Story of a New Zealand River*, but had thought that *The Passionate Puritan* wasn't up to much. However, he did suggest that Jane start on a

> 'long NZ novel... put in Dad's struggles; and show the new generation growing out of the old. Take the Rolland[sic] recipe; start yourself from the year one; and rely on character in scenery to pull you through... Serious, with comedy inwoven as it come; and no dirt. Write what you have seen and felt realistically

and dramatically – be a female David Copperfield. ...There's a market waiting for that book, and permanent sale.[12]

Allen Adair certainly has no 'dirt' in it, and as Jane herself said there was nothing in it that could upset even her mother. It wasn't an epic or even a long novel, but more a comment on people's expectations from one another. The book was reviewed well when it came out and although it lacks the innovative surprise that *The Story of a New Zealand River* has, the construction of the book is better. Next to her first novel, Jane said that it was her favourite book. New Zealanders in the 1920s, however, did not embrace their own literature. There was still a strongly held belief that for a novel to be worth reading, it needed to be set elsewhere and that New Zealand could not provide an interesting background for a good story. Consequently Jane did not earn much from this novel and the threepences were slow in coming from her home country. Yet it has been the only other one of her novels to be reprinted. At one time the novel lost its currency, when some feminists felt it dealt in an unsympathetic way with Marion, the wife of Allen Adair. However, other readers have felt a sympathy for the character. Jane had the ability to create characters which readers could relate to either in a positive or negative way. No one could read *The Story of a New Zealand River* and not be irritated at some stage by Alice, and although Marion is portrayed as a silly woman through much of the book, she does try to understand her position, even if in a limited way. *Allen Adair* was the last book Jane wrote with a New Zealand background.

By the end of 1925 Jane was ill, this time with an outbreak of boils. A combination of overwork and disappointment at the lack of success of her novel had brought her to a stage where she needed to get away for a rest. Leonard Moore, her agent at Christy and Moore, lent his house on the Welsh border for her to go away and recuperate. In fact, she had recurrent boils for three years. The first boil had started on her front shoulder blade, but the second was much worse as it 'jumped out beside my navel the size of a duck's egg. I had to discard corsets, hold up my abdomen when I moved, get a complete hot water outfit, and give the boil hot fomentations with boric lint, and plaster it with glycerine almost continuously for three weeks, while reading manuscript at the same time.'[13] Her holiday away meant she returned in better health, but she was to be plagued with boils for the rest of her time in London; at one stage she couldn't go out as she had six at the base of her spine. In conjunction with the boils Jane had a very salty taste in her mouth and she describes her whole body as feeling metallic. Despite her poor health she continued working, as she still had to support herself, and was now reading and reviewing an enormous number of books for her columns in the *Sun*.

In 1926 Jane's fifth book, *The Besieging City*, was published. This time it was set in New York. Aspects of the book were autobiographical – she always wrote what she knew about. It had a mixed reception from reviewers. The *Times Literary Supplement* reviewer wrote,

> The circle of people dissected in *The Besieging City* by Jane Mander (Hutchinson 7s6d) are cleverly studied and reproduced, but not one of them is sympathetically handled. The general impression retained is that the fabric of the book has been hurriedly woven in order to embed in the story some clever character sketches.

The review in *The British Australian and New Zealander* was better:

> In *The Besieging City* Miss Mander has changed her venue: instead of the simple life in New Zealand bush we have the high sophistication of New York City. A satisfactory book ... personally I don't know first-hand a thing about New York society but Miss Mander has made me feel as though I did.

The book has some of the vigour that is seen in *The Story of a New Zealand River* but which was missing in her other three novels. She captures the frenzy and hectic atmosphere of that city. Some of the characters are more complex than any she had written about before, and she did tentatively edge toward introducing a lesbian relationship between her heroine and one other character. She moved forward and then backed off, as if it were a topic too dangerous to pursue. It sits under the surface of the story, unresolved.

Interestingly, Jane later found that Rebecca West was also writing a novel on New York at the same time. Jane's was published before that of Rebecca West, but in a later conversation with West, she learnt that they had both suffered a breakdown while writing about that exhausting city. But whereas Rebecca had the means to rest and recuperate in the South of France, Jane could not afford that luxury and had to continue working despite her illness.

Once again however, her new book did not make a lot of money for her. She continued with writing articles and surviving the fogs and wet days of London. She still loved London, and said she found it 'safer, easier and more diverting' to live there, but there were times when she was homesick for the bush in the north of New Zealand:

> There are days of course when I think that the sight of a Kauri tree – but when I feel like that I walk round Westminster Abbey.[14]

CHAPTER ELEVEN

≈

The way of the writer is long and hard.
Jane Mander

Jane's skill at creating a calm and restful atmosphere about her meant that she soon had a close circle of friends visiting at her Cathcart Road flat. Australian writer Vernon Knowles said of Jane that she had a great genius for friendship, repeating what her friends in New York had already said. It seemed that she had an inexhaustible supply of sanity and commonsense: 'I was very fortunate in having her for a close friend in London; life for me there would have been quite impossible without her to rely upon for comfort and advice, for with all her other amiable traits, she is a very practical person; and I can recommend as well with enthusiasm, certain delectable dishes that she has served up in her flat in South Kensington on occasions that demanded special celebration.'[1] Eventually Jane became exasperated with Vernon. His first book *The Street of Queer Houses* had good reviews from Jane and other critics, but it appeared to go to his head and he spent the next years getting advances from publishers and either not delivering or, as in the case of John Lane, writing such a short poor novel it brought the publishers nothing. As time went by, Jane thought he became less and less interesting and more and more pompous (both sins worse than adultery, in Jane's mind).

Jane had started up a group for discussions on literature and art, and she and about a dozen other professional women would meet regularly at her flat. She also received an enormous number of requests from would-be writers in New Zealand, as to how to break into the literary world in London; as well she received their manuscripts. Mona Tracy, a New Zealand writer of children's stories, sent work to Jane for her opinion when she was reading for Christy and Moore. Jane's advice to her is down-to-earth and sensible, warning her that although Mr Moore had accepted a manuscript from Mona Tracy it did not mean that it would be published.

Jane's most constant and lasting friendship with a New Zealand writer, though, was with Monte Holcroft, probably best known now for his inimitable essays during his editorship of the *Listener*. When he went to see Jane at her Cathcart Road flat he was writing novels, and in his memoirs *The Way of a Writer*, Holcroft records his meeting with Jane:

I walked that evening to her flat in Cathcart Road ... Here I was received by a tall woman with features strongly defined, eyes that met mine with a steady, appraising look, and a warm handshake. She had picked up a trace of American accent in her years in New York, but her way with words – the vowels coming out as if with relish – was entirely her own. After tea and cakes and some general talk she questioned me about my plans for the future. I told her what I had already told Leonard Moore, that I proposed to earn my living by writing for the magazines. She shook her head doubtfully. 'My dear boy,' she said, 'you will be competing with all the best writers, people known as the authors of best-selling books'. I said hopefully that I had already sold a story in London, and one or two in the United States, she continued to look at me almost in sorrow. 'I hope,' she said, 'you have been able to bring a lot of money with you to London.' I told her I had a little less than sixty pounds. This seemed to make up her mind. 'My dear Monte,' she said decisively, 'you must go back to New Zealand while you still have the money to buy yourself a ticket.'[2]

Jane then went on to expound the difficulties of breaking into the competitive world of literature. She still received an allowance from her father and although it was small, it did mean that she was able to have a roof over her head and some food on the table. She told Monte that 'London was a beautiful and exciting place to be in if you had money and friends. If you were penniless and alone its indifference was crushing. In New Zealand she reminded me I had relatives, and was known. If she had to be short of money that was where she would want to be.'[3] But Jane admitted that she, too, was told many of the things she was now saying to young hopeful authors and that it hadn't made her change her mind.

The sixth of Jane's novels, *Pins and Pinnacles*, was published in 1928. She had tried something new – four people of different artistic temperaments and their interaction. It had been a difficult book to write. She once said,

Those of us who write books are haunted by characters who merge from that nebulous region at the back of our minds, characters who take hold of us and demand that we give them shape and form. I have just been through such an experience. I have had to entirely reconstruct the novel I am at present writing because in the middle of it some people I had never thought of at the beginning came in and obsessed my thoughts and became so vital that they crowded out the others and would not give me any peace till I put them in. These obtrusive fictions are far more real to me than the maid who comes and cleans my room and the people who live on the floors above and below me.[4]

Pins and Pinnacles was a book written under duress. She had to complete a contract she had with Hutchinson, and it was a period when she was suffering terribly from another outbreak of boils. Reading the book now, it seems bowed down with introspection and heavy-handed psychology.

The reviews referred to her 'technique' rather than to the excitement or interest of the novel, and despite Hutchinson marketing it with excerpts from reviews which said it was a 'wittily told story', and that the 'characters have originality and interest' the book sank with barely a ripple.

Jane had known for some time that she could not produce decent creative work and earn her living at the same time in what she refers to as 'the London dogfight',[5] so she gave up the idea of writing novels and took on a job which she thought would interest her more. She became the English editor of a new private printing press in Paris. Three of her friends from New York – Monroe Wheeler, Glenway Wescott and Lloyd Morris – had moved from New York to Paris to live. Glenway Wescott had written a book called *The Apple of the Eye* which was considered, when it was published in 1924, to be the finest first novel by an American in the twentieth century. Glenway was very handsome, and a wealthy American woman Barbara Harrison fell in love with him. Unfortunately for Barbara, Glenway was already in love with Monroe Wheeler, and the men had moved to Paris so they could be together quietly out of the American limelight. Such was Barbara's regard for Glenway and for Monroe, that she agreed to finance the printing press in Paris. It became known as Harrison of Paris. Barbara Harrison later married Glenway's brother. Monroe was the designer and typographer and Glenway had some of his original work published by this firm.[6] Harrison of Paris aimed at something new and less expensive in limited editions. They wanted to make a feature of illustrations and typography, as well as of fine printing, and in Paris printing was cheaper and more varied than in England; and they could also be in touch with the artistic bookmakers of France, Holland, Italy and Germany. Books from Harrison of Paris were entirely subscribed and eventually sold better in England than in America.

Jane liked France and had visited often. Lloyd Morris often stayed in France – either in Paris or Antibes – and once when he was recuperating from surgery, Rebecca West, who was recovering from a nervous breakdown, came and read to him each day. It was through Morris that Jane met James Joyce, and also the French writers Paul Morand, Cocteau, and Giraudoux. As well as being once more in the centre of an artistic milieu, Jane was now also involved with all aspects of creating exquisite books.

Jane was proof-reader for Harrison of Paris, editorial adviser, and saw work through the press. She read the proofs of all Harrison books and was very proud of being associated with such fine printing – Hutchinsons, her own publishers, had always produced her books badly.

A book that she was especially proud of was a production of Aesop's *Fables*. She spent much time in meticulous research looking at the original translation into English in the British Museum. From the old book she described in detail all that it held so that the new production could be as like as possible. Harrison of Paris kept the original spelling and old style phrases and the book was printed as a more faithful copy of the original than any made by any other press. Jane saw the whole publication through the press. The typesetters working on it were French, so the chances of typographical errors were immense. Jane would track them down, send the proofs back to the printers, then find more mistakes in the new lot and so back they went again. She was quick to spot new errors, and loved her game with the printers, making her instructions in dynamic French. The book was a huge success.

In spite of the world-wide financial crisis Harrison of Paris continued to produce beautiful books. Only at one stage were they forced to close the whole business down for about eighteen months because of the slump, but it started up again in 1930. The first book they produced was *Venus and Adonis*, the object being to produce a beautiful book rather than new subject matter; it was a graceful tribute by the Americans to Shakespeare. The second book was a collection of stories by Bret Harte. The colour illustrations were by a Frenchman, Pierre Falke; Jane kept a copy for her own collection, as she thought the illustrations were quite different from any English work she had seen. The French work she thought was less literal than the English, more subtle.

The three young men of Harrison admired Jane enormously. Monroe Wheeler thought her 'articulate and exuberant, tremendously enthusiastic for all she cared about and a person with enormous gusto', and he thought that she had the best literary taste. It was, he said, a great pity that she had never made any money from her books, for at the time her novels were being published she had a certain *succès d'estime*.[7]

As well as assisting with the work of Harrison of Paris, Jane continued writing her articles for the *Sun* in New Zealand and still read manuscripts for Christy and Moore, but London was becoming harder for her to survive. Once again she felt anguish at the noise and dirt of a large city, at the difficulty of making ends meet, and at the sheer frustration of trying to get her novels published. In 1931 she stayed in London through the winter and left for the country in the summer. Shropshire was the place she went to where she could work on her book. She spent that summer working on a new novel and did not read manuscripts for nearly a year. The relief of being able to work on her own creative material without the intrusion of reading lesser work by others improved her health. Once back in London though, she knew as soon as her novel went to her agents that she would be back on the treadmill of reading manuscripts in order to support herself.

By the end of 1931 Jane was flat broke. She would be 'hollering for work when I see Moore on Wednesday, though I do hate the thought of manuscript reading. I have been off it for a year thanks to help from my father.' There is the sound of depression in what she writes to her friends, and she bemoans the fact that hordes of clever young Oxford and Cambridge graduates were writing books, reviewing them and boosting each other. 'We outsiders have to be so much better than they to get any notice at all. I am in the depths of depression myself at present because I do not know what the fate of my last novel will be. ... Nobody knows better than I that the way of the writer is long and hard.'[8]

If the novel was not a success, she would have to return to New Zealand as she believed that she could not expect to rely on help from her father for too much longer. She was realistic enough to realise that she would miss her friends in England 'most dreadfully' but she wrote:

> I am really getting quite homesick for quiet and sunshine and scenery and the hills of my childhood. I should hate it in some ways, but like it in others. But I do need the publicity of a book or two to start me off as a writer out there, and so I am hoping to get another book that I have started finished before I come.[9]

She finished the two books and they were in the hands of her agent. Apart from her mentioning that she had to do some revision on one of them, no more is heard of them and the manuscripts have been lost. She had hoped that the books would bring her some publicity and some money so that she could return home. By the beginning of May she was admitting to being 'sick of London'. The people whose company she had enjoyed were no longer about and the others she found 'disappointing'. Apart from the music, and some plays and a few friends there was little in London to hold her. She reiterates in a letter to Monte Holcroft that she hungered for the sun and the smell and sights of her childhood. 'I really want to come back whether it is for good or not.'[10]

Four months later, in September, Jane Mander was on her way back to New Zealand. From the New Zealand Shipping Company's *Rangitiki* with the address 'In the Pacific' she wrote to Monte Holcroft. It is typical of Jane that the letter is full of encouragement for his writing, and she wishes she had some money not for herself but to help him over his period of dreadful poverty.

In a very revealing passage in the letter, Jane shows how hard it was to break into the literary world in London with the colonial background she had. The lack of a good solid classical education and all the contacts it brought, was never underestimated by her:

I so well understand the lack of a sophisticated background that causes writers like you and myself – both with a genuine impulse to write – to have to struggle a good while for technique. That is all you lack now – simply a finished technique for a book as a whole and you simply cannot help getting it with practise. Some of these clever young English writers are born with technique in their pens. They inherit it. But we overseas people do not and nothing in our youth helps us. It takes us longer of course to get the best publishers; but if you achieve one of them by the time you are 35 you will be doing very well. When you are depressed remember that Conrad and H.H. Richardson had to wait for 20 years (tho'[sic] they always wrote better than many who were recognised).[11]

She also applauded Holcroft's intention to keep himself to himself in order to write better:

Alas – I have wasted too much time on non-essentials – the world has been too much with me and I shall never do now what I might have done if I had thought more of my work. But I've enjoyed being gregarious, so I suppose that is compensation.[12]

Despite her feeling depressed at having to leave good friends behind in London, the six-week journey home to New Zealand was a break for Jane and the enforced rest allowed her health to improve. There was also time to work on her new book, and to contemplate the joy she would have of being able to revisit her beloved North. Once the ship crossed into the Pacific and she felt the warmth of the southern hemisphere, she was sure that the staleness she had felt in London would dissipate. The thought that she would again be able to go camping and boating, something she had always had a passion for, made her feel positive that under the benevolence of the North she would find fresh inspiration. In the back of her mind though was concern as to how she would find Aucklanders after such a long time away. She hoped that there would be at least one or two kindred spirits, after all she had some good introductions from London to all sorts of people in New Zealand, 'and doubtless I will find some of them interesting'.

Of major importance was the prospect of having the financial pressure taken off her so that she could get to work on a new book which she hoped would be better than anything she had written so far. Her family had said they were keen for her to keep on writing and had promised her absolute peace so she could work, and her father had promised to give her enough money to live on. But before Jane arrived back in New Zealand, her mother died. Janet Mander had suffered ill health for a long time; as a semi-invalid she had spent her later years in a wheeled chair. Jane would soon find that the well-meant promises from her family would never be fulfilled.

CHAPTER TWELVE

≈

I have wished myself out there many times
in the last year or two, for the country life
in the north is really very lovely. But
I suppose I should hate the people.
Letter to Monte Holcroft, 27 July 1931

When Jane arrived back in New Zealand in October 1932, she was fifty-five years old. Her hair was now grey and cut in a severe style, her face was described as clean cut and her head sharp and full of attack, and her voice was said to be 'like a seagull ... harsh and complaining'.[1] She was welcomed back to the country as a famous author who had made her mark overseas and now had the good sense to return home. She was interviewed for the *New Zealand Observer* and was complimented that she was without 'hauteur'. Apparently when D'Arcy Cresswell returned he had upset some people in New Zealand literary circles by telling them how the country should get its culture into trim.

Other travellers on the *Rangitiki* hadn't realised that this was 'the Jane Mander' – the famous author – she had seemed so down to earth. As Jane said, 'people haven't got over expecting poets and writers to wreathe their hair and go singing.'[2]

She was also interviewed by the *Auckland Star*, and said that she had been commissioned to write another novel of old New Zealand life. Once again, there is no trace of a manuscript for this novel. But she was buoyant and happy enough to say that she would certainly be writing and hoped she would make enough money to enable her 'to go Home occasionally'.[3]

In the interview Jane commented on how she admired New Zealand verse. However, she did not make any mention of New Zealand prose – at that time she had not received any hopeful writers' manuscripts to read. By December, she had been inundated with correspondence from writers all round New Zealand asking for advice. The work she saw appalled her. 'What is the matter with our would-be authors? Such crudity! Such sentimentality! Such triviality! Pathetic! For the verse reaches a much higher plane on the whole.'[4]

What was far more disturbing to her though, than the trash she was being sent to read, was the discovery that her father was not as well off as she had been led to believe. It was blatantly apparent that she would have to make as much money as she could at whatever she could do. True she did not have to worry about providing a place to live, but although that concern was removed she was immediately submerged by requirements from her family. She had been to visit relatives in the Waikato and in Whangarei and was then expected to provide for a large family reunion at Christmas. She once wrote that she loathed Christmas, and the burden on her to create a happy holiday atmosphere for her relatives just after arriving home was oppressive.

Already she was missing her friends in London, and felt very dislocated and apathetic. She wrote often to her friends overseas, and Monroe Wheeler remembers receiving letters from Jane which contained a thread of yearning, wishing to know what they were doing and what was happening in their lives.[5]

What Jane thought she would like would be a year's rest but this was not going to be possible. She didn't know what journalism she would try, but an introduction to John Schroder of the Christchurch *Press* meant there was an avenue to explore. She had also met up with Jock Gillespie, who had come to Auckland to be the editor of the *Sun*; when that newspaper collapsed he became editor of the *Mirror*. She was relieved to find him interesting and knowledgeable about literature and someone with whom she could at least have a good conversation. Jock Gillespie immediately offered Jane some freelance work in the new year for the *Mirror*. She also approached the Sydney *Bulletin* for work, it was 'light stuff' that was wanted, and she was really only interested on getting on with writing a novel, but it paid.

Warwick Lawrence, who was working at the *Mirror* when Jane began writing for it, remembers the first time he met her:

> My meeting with Jane Mander came about one afternoon when she called at The Mirror offices in Dilworth Building with the book reviews which Jock Gillespie had commissioned her to contribute each month. Jane liked to deliver her copy personally whenever possible to allow herself the opportunity of discussing books and book-men and life in general over a cup of tea with Jock in his cubby-hole of an office. She was a slim woman of middle height, she looked frail and cold, wrapped in a coat of dark blue with a fur collar and a matching hat of blue velvet. She carried her head high and looked more like the self-confident mistress of a girl's school than a writer of novels. I gained the impression that she was fairly pleased with herself, rather smug in fact. When she removed her hat I saw that her hair was white, cut close like a

≈ JANE'S HOME IN LONDON – 49 CATHCART ROAD, CHELSEA – AFTER SHE MOVED THERE IN 1923. PHOTOGRAPHED IN 1995.

≈ Jane as a London flapper in the 1920s. Courtesy of Judy Beetham

≈ Two photographs of Jane published in the *Mirror*, 1 January 1932, on her return to New Zealand.
Top left: Jane before she left in 1912.
Main picture: the returning novelist. Auckland Public Library

≈ A PORTRAIT OF JANE MANDER AS DISTINGUISHED NOVELIST, BY BARNES GRAHAM. AUCKLAND PUBLIC LIBRARY

man's, in a style we used to call an 'Eton Crop'. Later when I came to know Jane better I found that under that facade of smugness a sensitive, caring and helpful woman of strong personal convictions. I stood in awe of her. I addressed her, then and ever afterwards, as Miss Mander.'[6]

Jane would have been surprised that she was seen as smug. Her struggles throughout her life meant she was always well aware of the difficulties people faced each day, and was ready to help whenever she could. It may be that her look of sophistication and the briskness and brusqueness of her tongue intimidated people meeting her for the first time.

Jane also went to see Mr Hacket, the editor of the *New Zealand Herald* and suggested to him that she write an article on the Little Theatre Movement. In true Mander style, she spelt out to Mr Hacket exactly what she required. She wanted two guineas for the piece if it were published. She did not want any editorial cuts, and if the editor did think it should be cut (and the implication here is that editorial interference would be rash) she would rather have the article returned than have it chopped about. Her third demand was that she would like to be advised early as to whether the paper was going to accept the piece, because if they weren't going to publish it within the next week she would then offer it to someone else. It is typical of Jane that she would make such definite demands, but there is also a feeling of urgency in her instructions – she needed the work, she needed the money.

By March of 1933 Jane had started on her radio talks. She was initially contracted to present a dozen and they covered such topics as Modern Book Productions, Living Conditions in New York and London, Art Galleries and Museums. She found this an easy way to make money, and it was good publicity for her, too. Even though each talk was to be for twenty minutes' duration, they didn't take long to write and she enjoyed the work. When she broadcast them she had a fascinating voice, with a slight American accent that sounded good on radio.

Jane also joined the guest speaker circuit, and spoke at many women's groups and clubs. In a talk she gave to the Lyceum Club in June 1933 she spoke of well-known people she had met when she was overseas. Much of the talk is a list of famous people of the day, but she does mention a visit she made to Washington at the end of the war:

> Through the Red Cross work I met many Washington people, and when the peace conference was on after the war was over I went to Washington as the guest of the William Mather Lewis's. He was the assistant secretary of the Treasury, and at parties in their house I met all the diplomatic people of Washington. I was at a reception given by Mr Mellon the secretary, and was more thrilled by his magnificent collection of pictures than I was by the

celebrities present. Then the Minister for Education, Mr Capin, who had read my *Story of a New Zealand River*, gave me dinner at the Chevy Chase Club, and told me that on the first holiday he could get he would come to visit New Zealand on my descriptions of its scenery. I saw from the inside on that visit what is meant by the glamour of diplomatic society for those that like it. It was a brilliant three weeks but it nearly killed me – it was so strenuous.

These speaking engagements were useful for Jane – they kept her name to the fore in the public mind, and provided a small income. But her energy was dissipated, and the whole intention of writing another novel had to be pushed to one side. She had always thought that both *Allen Adair* and *The Besieging City* were written too quickly, and she almost dismissed *Pins and Pinnacles* because its birth was purely to fulfil contractual obligations. She felt that she needed to justify whatever promise there was in her writing in *The Story of a New Zealand River*, and that would mean concerted concentration, but there was no hope of that until her finances improved.

Jane felt overwhelmed by her family. She said, 'I'm dying to get on with another book, but my family is a terrible detainer.'[7] Although she complained about not being able to work on her novel because of her family's need of her, she was very concerned about her family responsibilities, and when her sister-in-law, whom she loved, became ill, it was Jane who went to look after her. When, after some time caring for her sister-in-law she arrived home to her eighty-four year-old father, there was no chance to rest. Still a man of enormous energy he had decided that they would move from 48 Ranfurly Road and so began rushing about looking for somewhere to live. He insisted on driving a car and would race down Remuera Road between the tramlines oblivious to oncoming traffic and pedestrians. The family made him promise to stop driving when he was ninety, and when he turned ninety he said he still had a year to go until he was 91 – ever the politician. Jane was constantly worried about his well-being, and could not settle to any creative work. 'Really one has no peace in a family. What a weird thing it is that every creative artist has this trouble with relatives.'[8] She did admit, though, that all the concern with her family meant that her head had a rest and she finally began to feel more mentally fit than she had for a long time. She was again reading manuscripts and still finding that the level of novel writing was poor:

> No one out here seems to have the remotest notion of the standard of prose writing in London, and what these would-be novelists read I cannot imagine, that they think such stuff could be publishable. You [Monte Holcroft] are a literary genius beside all this stuff – so take heart.[9]

In May Jane was still writing to Monte Holcroft about how hard up she was – not because she wanted to have more money for herself, but because there was nothing spare to give to the Holcrofts, who were experiencing dire poverty at the time. Perhaps her father believed he had helped her enough, for he paid out two thousand pounds so that her sister Annie could make changes to the house she had bought for a hospital which was known as Mt Pleasant, but in the six months Jane had been home she had been given nothing. It seemed absurd to Jane that someone with as many properties as her father could be so short of cash. But it was the tail end of the depression and the people who rented the properties Frank Mander owned couldn't pay their rent, and he would not turn them out. What this meant was that the Mander household had to make certain economies and one was to dispense with the housekeeper. Jane of course then became the domestic. The only income she had was from her radio talks, which she gave every three weeks.

Despite these aggravations Jane still had time to write to Monte Holcroft and urge him on. She was prepared to read his manuscripts and offer her opinions, and was appalled on one occasion when she learned that he could not afford to post her the manuscript. She was so convinced of his talent that she wrote to her literary agent in London, who was also Holcroft's agent, promoting his work. At one stage she suggested that he should apply for relief work and was told it was not an option he could accept as he was determined to become a published writer. Jane fully understood this and probably admired him even more for his stance.

Her father finally got his wish and sold the house in Ranfurly Road and bought another at 10 Keith Avenue in Remuera. They moved in only to find that all the pipes leaked and so the whole of the inside of the house had to be redone. As a further economy, Frank Mander decided that Jane's sister Carrie, who had been living in a special home, would come and live with them. Jane described her as 'eccentric and a terrible trial'. Other members of the family have since described Carrie as 'fey', but another relative said the problem with Carrie was that her father had insisted she ride horses which were not properly broken in when she was a young girl, and fell on her head too often. Whatever the reason for Carrie's state of mind, she was to come and live in the house with Jane and her father, and a room had to be built on to the house to accommodate her.

For Jane it was a terrible situation, she could see there would be no peace for her and contemplated whether she could get enough work to keep herself elsewhere. Though the Holcrofts were so poverty stricken Jane had a small feeling of envy. 'I would rather be in a tiny room somewhere and have leisure than be here I can tell you.'[10] There was no hope of her getting down to any serious writing, for not only was she doing all the housework, and the gardening, but her father liked her to entertain him by playing cards with him each evening, which she found boring and a waste of time. She was promised that the next year she would get some money from an investment, so she was biding her time. As she said in her letters to Monte Holcroft, she did have a house, and food and all the clothes she needed for a while, and she managed to sneak her tramcar fares out of the housekeeping. In the midst of all this economic and emotional disruption, Jane continued to display her generosity by sending her hard-earned money to the Holcrofts.

> I made up my mind weeks ago that most of the money I got for a November article in the Mirror should come to you for Christmas as a small donation towards the difficult business of living. Then I decided a few days ago that there was no need to wait for Christmas when other people might do something, that perhaps you desperately needed something now, and so today, when in town I got the notes ready to post off with a letter tonight. I only wish I could afford fifty instead of this small sum.[11]

As well as sending money, Jane continued to send good advice. When Monte Holcroft finished his book *African Tale* he sent it to Jane for her comments. Her response was quick and positive:

> I am thrilled to be able to tell you that you have written a good book and one far ahead of anything you have so far done ... It is so refreshingly away from the 'rut' of 'modern' books and so finely in the spirit of universal human life and problems that it ought to draw the thoughtful public ... I find both tale and setting entirely convincing, and I am lost in admiration of the vividness with which you present a life and a setting of which you really could not have seen very much when you were in Africa. This is a creative work, and though books set back in time may show that the author is escaping from his own day and age, still you are not escaping from life in this ... I don't want to encourage you too much ... but I do feel that this will start you in a new direction. There is a quiet power and thought behind it, as well as your excellent story sense, and the writing is genuinely beautiful in so many places that I feel it must get a first-rate publisher.[12]

The Holcrofts valued such support and Ray Holcroft, Monte's wife, was to say of Jane Mander that she knew modern novels better than anyone else in New Zealand.[13] And when Holcroft decided that in order to make some money he would have to forgo writing novels and move into essay writing, Jane understood his reasons and supported him in that decision too. 'Why should not your writing gift be a versatile one.'[14]

Jane continued to be inundated with manuscripts from hopeful novelists. She was well-known through her radio talks and the fact that she was a published author who had experienced the literary world of London and New York made her an obvious target. She was surprised at the numbers of people – mostly women – who were trying to write fiction. It seemed to her that every town had its own writers club, and at the end of a day of domestic activity women were settling in to write 'the novel'. Unfortunately although the clatter of typewriters and the scratch of pens filled the air, there seemed in Jane's opinion to be little improvement in writing in New Zealand since she had left twenty years before.

The appalling nature of the work she was receiving goaded her into writing a series of articles for *The Press*. Entitled 'New Zealand Novelists – An Analysis and Some Advice' the articles were probably the first clearly detailed advice published for aspiring local writers. Jane was so keenly interested in literature that she wanted to encourage and support new young talented writers, but she could not see that even one of the manuscripts sent to her had potential. She maintained that New Zealand's education system had produced the 'New Stupid', a term she borrowed from Aldous Huxley: 'a half-baked, wrongly-educated, pretentious, cinema-polluted mongrel lot'[15] was how she described the writers she was reading.

'Why do these "New Stupid" want to write?' she asks and then answers her own question with scorn that most of them say that they want to make money. Jane, who had first-hand knowledge of how little a writer made from writing, was scathing. 'The people who write for money will never raise the standard for literature in New Zealand.' She goes on to write, 'There is only one way to interesting writing, to glamorous writing, to great writing and that way is hard work, constant practice, the study of good models, the reading of poetry – hard work tempered by humility, moral courage, and the willingness to take criticism, and enlivened by a grand variety of mental growing pains.'

The three articles appeared over three weeks, and much of the advice is as useful today as it was then. Her discussion of 'style' is typically frank: 'our writers may have, and indeed, often do have, a very respectable story sense. They have the gift of description, probably the best arrow in the quiver so far. But they lack style, distinctive expression, a sense for words, a sense for rhythm.'

In an article also written for *The Press,* Ngaio Marsh applauded the articles:

Miss Jane Mander's articles on the New Zealand novel come in good season. If she writes with all the exasperation of one who has been balked of an interesting rendezvous, yet her exasperation is not amiss. One is reminded of the treatment that is occasionally given to new-born babies who have difficulty in breathing. The infant is seized upon by mid-wife and accoucheur, violently swung to and fro, submitted to scientific buffeting, tossed up and down, and knowledgeably slapped until it draws breath and takes life. Miss Mander's energy tempts one to liken her to a sort of literary mid-wife and to hope that the inert infant may respond with a lusty howl.

It is when she deals with the technical problems of the New Zealand novel that I find her most enthralling. Among others I have tried to write such a novel and have at once found myself confronted by difficulties as great as they are hard to define. Miss Mander has defined them and anything that I may add will be no more than a footnote to her articles.[16]

An observation Jane made in one of the articles is still unfortunately true:

It is more than astonishing, it is lamentable, that people in authority over art institutions often don't know anything of their subject, but would reject a book because it had an unpleasant scene in it, or because it dealt with a controversial subject. The city fathers want books to be 'moral' without any knowledge of what morality in art is.

In her concluding article she closes by saying:

By degrees after study, some magic works in the mind of the genuine artist, words sing to him ease comes to him (comparative ease that is, for to some creation is never easy) and he finds himself carried along where previously he had to stumble. And I might add in concluding this article that a genuine creative gift is almost invariably accompanied by a strange humility, by something as far removed as possible from the complacent childlike delusion of the majority of our scribblers that their wordiness has anything to do with art.

Jane's own artistic struggle was bogged down by domestic and family interference. The energy she poured out in assisting other writers meant her store was depleted. By the end of 1933 she still had not managed to complete any new work which she could regard as 'serious'.

CHAPTER THIRTEEN

≈

What a trial it is to be a writer. We need
special niches, every one of us.
Letter to Monte Holcroft, 17 May 1934

Jane had received no money from her father since she had been back from England; perhaps because of this Frank Mander decided that he would take her on a trip to the South Island. The whole idea was sprung on her as a surprise; as she was trying to work on her novel at the time, she would have preferred that her father went on his own and left her in peace to continue writing. However, she agreed to go with him.

It is testament to her father's stamina and determination that at the age of eighty-five the itinerary he had planned was exhausting. They were to travel from Auckland to Wellington and on to Invercargill, back to Queenstown and on to Cromwell and Christchurch, staying only one night in each place.

Half-way through the trip Jane caught a cold and had to forgo some of the chasing around her father had organised. She stayed at Lake Wakatipu until she felt better. On arrival in Christchurch, she and her father were to stay with a relative who was a Wesleyan Parson: Jane made it very clear that she was not going to be tied down to sitting around with dreary relatives. She arranged to meet Monte Holcroft at his home. 'I beg you not to try to get anything special for me', she wrote 'and don't imagine I shall mind whether you live in one room or twenty. Didn't I live for years in London in one room?'

She spent a day walking on the Cashmere Hills with Monte and Ray Holcroft discussing art and literature and the difficulties inherent in trying to get work published. She returned to Auckland with some of Holcroft's work and managed to get Jock Gillespie to publish 'the River Craft', and a couple of other stories Holcroft had written, in the *Mirror*. As well, Jock Gillespie, who was definitely a good friend to Jane, had wangled a book page for her in that same magazine. She had a free hand and could write about any books she liked, which was much better than merely reviewing books sent to the magazine by publishers. She was pleased to get the work; it meant she could do her own reading, and get two guineas for the article.

The trip also gave Jane an opportunity to call in and see John Schroder at *The Press*. The visit was useful and she returned from her journey south with a commission for some articles.

She worked hard on the articles on her return to Auckland but despaired at getting back to writing novels. Once again the house at Keith Avenue was filled with relatives. Finally Jane demanded that she have two quiet hours in the morning to get on with her work, if this demand was not accepted, she would leave them all to it. It was a threat which shot home – the unpaid nurse, housekeeper, gardener and cook was talking of leaving! Her father still had not given her any money and she regarded him as a pathological miser. Her anger at him never abated and she raged every day against her fate. Her income was wholly derived from what she could earn on the *Mirror* and elsewhere. With the necessity of having to expend energy on writing for magazines, Jane began to feel left behind with her serious literary work, and commented to Monte Holcroft that 'the new novels coming out are all so clever, so up-to-date, so dramatically in the present world.'[1] She thought that she was not writing very inspiringly, and was depressed and disgruntled. She longed for a place of her own, but her father bribed her with the promise that she would eventually inherit money from him if she stayed and looked after him now. Of course she had no idea that her father would live until he was ninety-four, and that she had another nine years of coping with his crankiness.

Despite her personal discontent with her writing, Jane's articles still reflect her sharp mind, and the prodigious amount of work she did for her book page was remarkable. In one month she read twenty-two books. She saw that the reading market had changed over the previous ten years. She wrote to Holcroft, 'It's sad for people like us outsiders who have no footing in England and no publicity to help us but we've got to face facts.' The 'facts' were that unless the book was set in England or in Europe, there was no chance for it to be accepted by an English publishing house. Facing facts, Jane had decided that her new novel was going to be set in England, on the Welsh border where she had spent 'two enchanting summers', she wanted it to be modern and up-to-date, and had set it in 1932. She wrote and told Monte Holcroft that it was going to be 'as Bright as a Button'. He wrote back to her in horror at the thought of her writing something which sounded so flippant. She soothed his fears that she had lost her interest in writing serious fiction and replied, 'It has nothing to do with London or ephemeral cults and fashions ... it is apart from the world while being of it – and I did a third of it or thereabouts before leaving England. It must be done before I go back to the New Zealand setting which of course I am going to do later.'[2]

The manuscript for this novel has disappeared, and it is not known if it was ever completed.

By the end of 1934 Jane was exhausted. She had set herself a huge task of reading for the page in the *Mirror*, but had also been engulfed with spring cleaning and sewing. She remarked again to Monte Holcroft that her life was hardly worth thinking about, and that the only redeeming feature was that she would not starve. Despite her continual worries with earning a living she still managed once more to send money to Monte Holcroft and his wife that Christmas.

After Christmas she managed to have a break away, and be by herself to rest. She travelled up to the Bay of Islands and camped. She lay in the sun, swam, read and relaxed. It was what she had hoped for when she had decided to return to New Zealand. At the end of the summer though, Jane was again in a state of frustration. She had been overburdened with relatives to stay and as well had taken on that domestic chore so endorsed by every Women's Institute throughout New Zealand, bottling fruit! Her sense of futility made her feel suicidal, and the only thing she could do which helped was to read.

By now Jane was well established with the literary group such as it was in New Zealand. She visited the cottage in Castor Bay where D'Arcy Cresswell, Frank Sargeson and Iris Wilkinson (Robin Hyde) would meet. This has often been seen as the literary centre of Auckland at the time, but in fact Jane did not go there regularly, though in June 1938 she wrote that she was off to Castor Bay for a week.[3] Most of the writers Jane knew were too poor to take the trip across to Castor Bay, and Sargeson used to walk there along the beach from Takapuna.

Jane was always desperately concerned at the fate of the writers she knew and voiced her concern to Holcroft:

> *All the struggling boys up here have had to get regular work. Fairburn is doing some routine job in Farmers, Coppard is in a woolshed, R.A.K. Mason is doing some stupid office work. D'Arcy Cresswell is in a hut out on the beach somewhere living on his radio talks – and so it goes. It is all wrong.*[4]

When she could, she helped these 'boys' and at one time Frank Sargeson would cross over from Takapuna on the ferry to work in the Mander garden. The job had originally been offered to Harry Doyle, Frank's close friend, but in the end it was Frank who took it on. He would supply plants for the garden, as well as help Jane with weeding and general tidying.

He had sent her a copy of *Conversation with My Uncle* in the hope that she would review it in the *Mirror*. Jane thought that Sargeson's 'sketches', as she called them, were the best of their kind done by any New Zealander, but she couldn't review such a slight book because the *Mirror* had cut back her space. 'If I reviewed small books of your kind I should be deluged with them. So I have to refuse them as I cannot make distinctions.'[5]

Frank Sargeson referred to Jane as 'a terrifically good old scout'.[6] She believed wholeheartedly in Sargeson's talent and enjoyed his company, otherwise she would not have bothered with him. She was tolerant of his eccentricities because she valued him as an artist. As they gardened they would talk, and Jane often lent books from her own collection so that Sargeson could keep up to date with his reading. The gardening day would include a good lunch, so that he would not have to bother about an evening meal.

Later she became very concerned about Sargeson's health. She had no money so could not give him any more work in the garden, but she was very concerned that he was not eating properly. She wrote and suggested that if he was in a hole financially he was to let her know and she would borrow some money off her sister. 'For God's sake don't be such a fool as to starve. I insist on getting you to a diet man if you are no better for a milk diet for a week.'[7] They remained friends until her death.

In 1935 Jane became involved with organising the New Zealand Authors' Week, which was to take place in April of 1936. Part of this week was the compilation of a book which listed New Zealand authors and their publications, with photos of representative writers, some poetry, and a few articles. Three thousand copies were to be printed; at the time it was published, the book was the most complete anthology on New Zealand writers. The hope of the organising committee was that the book would not only be attractive, but that it would be useful too. Jane's job was to see that the writers she knew personally sent in their lists of publications and their biographies. It was a frustrating job and she was particularly irritated with D'Arcy Cresswell and Iris Wilkinson. In a letter to Johannes Andersen she said of Cresswell and Wilkinson,

> They are both inclined to think they should be sought out, which is absurd in this case as I have told them. It would be a pity to have them left out, as they are undoubtedly two of the most significant of our living creative artists. Robin Hyde may indeed be the greatest living poet we have produced. I also learned yesterday that R.A.K. Mason had not sent any word of himself. He

has written some strong verse and should be included in any New Zealand anthology. But if he won't make the effort to comply with conditions he will have to be left out. These temperamental people are often very childish.[8]

As well as listing publications from New Zealand authors, the book included a section on book plates. Jane had joined the Ex Libris society on her return to New Zealand and one of her bookplates was included. It was a wood-cut done by Stephen F. Champ, showing fantails flirting around a river with logs about to cascade. In the note relating to the woodcut Johannes Andersen wrote. 'The whole suggests A New Zealand River, the title and theme of the first and we think the best of the owner's novels – a personal touch which gives a great interest to a vigorously-executed plate.'[9]

When asked to comment on this statement before the book went to print, Jane agreed that *The Story of a New Zealand River* was her best book so far, but added that she was hoping to write a better one, and 'justify my greater experience of writing and of life.'[10]

For the moment though, Jane could not contemplate settling down to completing her novel. Still short of money, 'My father grows more miserly every day. It is a disease of the very old',[11] she began to consider doing regular book reviewing on the radio. It meant that she would have to read what she considered 'a lot of tripe for the mob' books which she admitted she would not normally read for herself, and it also meant that she would not be able to do any extra writing. As it was, throughout the winter of 1935 Jane had been troubled with what she referred to as neuritis in her right arm – what we today would diagnose as Occupational Overuse Syndrome. It had been so painful that she could not even cut bread, and her sister Carrie had to help her more, which was no bad thing. The great disadvantage was that typing was out of the question, so that all her writing now had to be done by hand. For twenty years she had typed everything. In the end she had to go to Whangarei to stay with her sister Tommy in order to rest her arm, but even that had no effect. She had to return to Auckland for some elaborate electrical treatment which she had three days every week for several months. Even though it was extremely painful to write anything, good friend that she was, she managed a short note to Monte Holcroft to tell him how thrilled she was that his book *The Papuan* had been highly commended in the S.H. Prior Memorial Prize and was to be serialised in *The Bulletin.*

Once again in her Christmas letter to the Holcrofts Jane sent money for 'anything you want extra for the family Xmas.' Always delighted when a writer received the acknowledgement she thought they deserved, Jane commented in the same letter on Iris Wilkinson having two books accepted in London. 'She has real gifts and now I hope will be on the road to success.' She also passed on news of D'Arcy Cresswell and R.A.K. Mason. Apparently Cresswell had gone to do one of his radio talks boozed and had been cut off; it was fairly unlikely that he would be asked to talk on radio again, and so he had lost his only source of income, 'Crazy crazy,' Jane wrote. On the other hand, R.A.K. Mason was publishing a booklet of sonnets which Jane thought were far too obscure for most New Zealanders and at a price of five shillings too dear for the rest.

In February of 1936 Monte Holcroft was in the most dire poverty. He telegraphed the only person he knew from whom he could borrow money. Jane immediately responded and followed up with a very graceful letter saying that it was not inconvenient for her to send the money, and that she was glad she could do it. She also told him that he need not return it as 'you are evidently having a hard time at the moment. At present I am making a bit extra by talking over the radio, and after this series of five is finished I shall begin to read for another to be given later on in the winter. Also I have one to do for Authors' Week. And I imagine I shall be able to go on indefinitely with various series after due intervals.'[12]

It was typical of Jane's generosity and kindness that she should show in the letter that she had plenty of work and was not as hard-up as she had been, and that she did have money coming in, and was seemingly able to spare the amount she sent to the Holcrofts. She concludes the letter by saying 'Don't think any more of the money. I am glad to help you, and I know how hard things can be at times. If I had more only too gladly would I help poor artists.'[13]

After nearly a year on the committee organising Authors' Week Jane was looking forward to the publication of the book, and keen to see that the week which was to be devoted to promoting New Zealand writers was successful. She had agreed to give a talk on Post War New Zealand Authors, but it was a sign of her frazzled nerves and her domestic load – it was February and she was bottling peaches again – that she had to write and ask Monte Holcroft to send her a list of all his books published in London. She admits in the letter that she could not remember the titles. In preparing her talk, Jane suddenly found that there were many New Zealand writers whom she had never read. She decided that she could skip reading all of Nelle Scanlan's novels, even though she would of course mention her in the list. Jane had always thought Scanlan a lightweight populist writer. She had a formidable task, reading a huge number of books in order to give a talk which was representative of New Zealand authors, and then to have something concrete to say about them all.

It was an accomplished talk. She began by saying how surprised she had been to learn that since 1918 forty-six bona fide New Zealand authors had published 113 novels. She divided the authors up from those who had written more than two books since the first World War, down to the people who had written two books and one book. The talk is a comprehensive and interesting look at New Zealand writers in the 1920s and 1930s.[14] Some of the writers she listed were Rosemary Rees, Jean Devanny, Nelle Scanlan, Mrs Cluett, Elizabeth Milton (Rosemary Rees' sister), Sheila Macdonald, Ngaio Marsh, C.R. Allen, Monte Holcroft, Hector Bolitho, Dulcie Deamer, Walter Smyth, Scobie Mackenzie, Alice A. Kenny, Martin Stuart, Robin Hyde, and John A. Lee.

The talk also includes a paragraph in which Jane talks of the books she likes to read:

> In my personal taste I am that possibly alarming creature, a highbrow. When I wish to enrich my experience of art I want the greatest fiction I can get in the world. But – I do not wish to perch on the glittering mountain peak all my days. No more than anybody else can I be improving my mind all the time. I must be entertained and diverted, and amused sometimes. So must we all. So that while I wish to see better literary work in this country I am not denying the merits of our writers of light romance, of our writers of adventure, of our writers of thrillers. All we need to ask of them is that they do their job well. Some of them do.

Her friends Monte Holcroft, Robin Hyde and John A. Lee have the most glowing reviews, and she goes so far as to say that she would hold John A. Lee's novel *Children of the Poor* as the best novel she had read, on account of its power and courage. But she can't resist an oblique swipe at Nelle Scanlan, 'Though lacking distinction, Miss Scanlan's style is breezy and vigorous and her vitality remarkable. She is fortunate in having gifts entirely acceptable to the majority of readers in her own country in her lifetime.'

But as well as being critical of other authors' work, Jane also admits that her own standard of work fell far short of what she thought it ought to be. 'If I could begin my writing career over again I feel I should write very differently. And feeling this way about my own work I can without offence, I hope, point out some faults in our fiction. First of all we lack distinction, a feeling for style, a gift for the sensitive choice of words. We lack the rich equipment of the best English writers.'

Authors' Week was a huge success. For the first time in New Zealand, writers were talked about and books were displayed throughout the country, bringing an awareness that there was a literary world that was maybe not yet blooming, but at least was alive and struggling to be seen and read.

As often happened when she had worked hard and put a lot of energy into a project, Jane finished the week feeling tired and jaded. The enormous amount of rush reading she had done for her talk left her feeling upset; she said her nerves were frayed. As well, it often seemed to happen that when Jane was busiest with her literary work the domestic world tended to fall apart. During Authors' Week Carrie, her sister who was mentally unwell, became worse than she had been for a long time; in order to get some respite, Jane spent some of her time at her niece Riro's house in St Heliers. It meant that she felt quite dislocated going backwards and forwards between houses, but the dislocation was eminently preferable to the chaos in the house with her father and her sister. Her father had been ill with 'flu and had become even more tiresome and demanding. Finally Jane began to contemplate getting someone to come and look after him, which would ease the burden she was expected to carry.

Jane had been working on some more talks for the radio, on Women Down the Ages, but in 1936 there was a great upheaval with the Broadcasting Board, something that seems to have been inherent in Broadcasting for the past sixty years. Alan Mulgan, whom Jane knew through their connections with the Pickmeres in Whangarei, was the Supervisor on the Broadcasting Board; she tried unsuccessfully to get in touch with him to find out whether she was going to have any work in the future, or whether the restructuring would mean cutting back on freelance work. She admitted that she wasn't too perturbed when she couldn't find anything out, as she had reached a point where she didn't care if she never spoke on radio again. She was keen to unload everything so that she could work on her book; although Authors' Week had left her feeling physically tired, she felt that her mind was fresher than it had been for some time. In fact, when the Broadcasting Board finally settled down again, Jane did give the talks she had prepared.

Ill health conspired once more against her getting to work on her novel. The neuritis in her arm continued to give her trouble. Treatment for this continued over a period of months, during which time she could neither type nor write, but then she had a problem with her eyes, which became so painful that she could not read. Added to all this was an uproar in the house while some redecorating was done and a new stove and califont were installed. Into this bedlam came the annual visit of relatives. For Jane it was hell revisited. She could stand it only with the knowledge that in January she would be able to go camping in her beloved North.

CHAPTER FOURTEEN

≈

One looks in vain for any collective aid
for the genuine artist.
Jane Mander, 'New Zealand Novels'[1]

In 1935 there was a change of government in New Zealand, with a Labour government voted in. It was hoped that some form of cultural support would come from the new administration. Many of the new Labour Members of Parliament were people with little formal schooling, who had attended WEA courses and read prodigiously to educate themselves. There was a climate emerging which showed some respect for writers and scholars and acknowledged that some form of recognition should be made. In the first few years that Labour was the Government, it granted pensions to Jessie Mackay, William Satchell, Eileen Duggan, and James Cowan. Those to Mackay, Satchell and Cowan were given on compassionate grounds, as they were elderly and unwell. Eileen Duggan received hers under a different category, because she was thought to be 'a lady of retiring and delicate character'[2] (whatever that was supposed to mean). But any assistance to the young artists struggling to be heard was not forthcoming.

For all the young authors Jane knew, such as Sargeson, Mason, Fairburn and Holcroft there was no financial help, and she continued as a one-woman support for those she could assist. She did her best to promote John A. Lee's book *Children of the Poor* and gave it a good review in her *Mirror* page. She was pleased that Labour had been elected to Parliament as she was always on the side of the young and the underdog, and welcomed new ideas. She was keen to see what the new style of government would bring, and also hoped that there would be some social policies implemented which would help those caught in the web of poverty, something about which she had first-hand knowledge. Amazingly, she had even persuaded her father that he should keep an open mind about the Labour Government. The conversation between Frank Mander who had been an MP with the Reform party, and his daughter with definite Socialist leanings must have been dynamic, particularly as Labour had ousted the Coalition government which had been made up of the Reform and United (formerly Liberal) parties. Obviously Jane's political powers of persuasion had not lessened. She said in a letter to John A. Lee,

> Certainly I have no sympathy with the old gang who would never have made a move to do for the poor what the government of little Savage has done. I admire his spirit, and I wish you every success in your work, and that is sincere.[3]

She had taken her copy of *Children of the Poor* when she went camping in Whangarei and lent it to her sisters and her niece whom she described as a 'pleasant flapper'; she was surprised and pleased to see that both her sisters and her niece were roused by the book. As soon as she was back in Auckland she wrote to Lee to tell him of their response to his work, and concluded her letter with words of encouragement for him as well as a bit of advice – Jane often took the opportunity to mix the two!

> I still feel John Lee that you have unique talent for writing, and that you are far and away our most powerful modern writer. Do go on with it. I am also entirely in sympathy with your housing scheme, and with the legislation of your party. More power to it.[4]

John Lee wrote to Jane and thanked her for the review she did of his book, and she replied in her usual direct way that he was not to thank her at all for what she had said because the review was just what she had honestly felt about the book and it was not a 'friend's' review.

It was unlikely, though, that she received any 'thank you' letter from Robin Hyde following the review she did of *Passport to Hell.* Jane was very disappointed with the book. She thought it had none of the beauty she saw in Hyde's poetry; she had always regarded Hyde as one of the best poets in New Zealand. She wrote that the book had no spiritual significance, and that in its way it was a fake. After such strong words the friendship between Hyde and Mander cooled. Jane was adamant that as a reviewer it was important that she preserve her detachment and give what she saw as an honest opinion. Yet like all writers she was defensive when critics attacked her work, even when she knew there were probably deficiencies. Such is the writer's ego.

Jane's own struggle continued, she was now writing for the *Mirror* and *The Monocle* as well as preparing more material for radio talks. The continued lack of money dogged her, and she was surprised to meet a young woman who told her that she was earning two pounds per week working freelance, writing for the *Auckland Star*, the *New Zealand Herald* and a magazine. But for Jane the idea of each week whipping together a saleable article for the newspapers was too awful for her to consider. She regarded herself as a serious artist; it already bothered her that she dissipated her energy reviewing and writing articles, however thoughtful she made them, merely to earn money.

In 1936 she resigned from the *Mirror* page. Henry Kelliher and Jock Gillespie were at odds over how the page should appear. Jane thought that Kelliher was not interested in the book page at all, and she had kept on working only to please Jock Gillespie, and of course for the money. The amount of reading she was having to do was worrying her eyes, and she decided that she would have to forego the money in order to conserve her eyesight. The stress at home had not diminished. Her father had been sick again, and was cranky and demanding. Carrie was still with them and was of no help in the running of the household. Added to this was a long wet Auckland winter which left Jane feeling very miserable and depressed.

She had started in a rather lacklustre way to prepare her second series of radio talks which would go to air in October and November. After that she had decided that she would not undertake anything further 'of a public nature'. She hoped that she would be able to 'play about' through the summer and get herself both mentally and physically fit so that she could come back and work on another book. The summer started off wet and dismal, campers were washed out of their tents and Jane's planned holiday on the Whangarei Harbour looked like it was doomed. However, finally in mid-January the weather improved and at last she could leave for three weeks of relatively idle time. It was a chance for her to rest her eyes, to swim and walk and talk with the family members she loved – her sister Tommy and her nieces. It was a restorative time. When she came back to Auckland, the North had worked its magic on her and she was ready to take on some work. While she had been away on holiday she had changed her mind about radio work, and had decided she could do some more talks, this time though she made it clear to the Broadcasting Service that she would not be rushed into anything and the talks would not be ready until June or July of 1937.

The domestic chores did not lessen, now added to the perennial bottling was the care of the garden, for Jane had started growing flowers for her sister's hospital. At least when she was working in the garden her eyes were resting, and although she still raged at not being able to write she felt relieved that she was not reading for the *Mirror* page. While she had been on holiday she had read Tolstoy's *War and Peace*, it impressed her so much that she thought that she would never read an 'ordinary novel' again, let alone write one.

Despite her sworn intentions that she would never read for the *Mirror* again, by the middle of the year Jane was back reading for the book page. The disagreements between Kelliher and Jock Gillespie appeared to have been resolved, and she thought that her eyes had been rested enough for her to take on the work again. At the same time she was made a very tempting offer by the Broadcasting Service. They wanted her to share in the running of a women's programme. It was an interesting offer, as the producers could create the programme in almost any way they pleased, and an added inducement was the pay which was two guineas a week. Jane gave it serious thought, but in the end she had to concede that life at home was too difficult for her to manage a regular job and cope with her father and a sister, whom she now openly referred to as 'mad'. She did agree however, to give talks on a casual basis on the radio. These were to be for about a ten minute duration, and for these she would be paid one guinea.

1937 was also the year that Jane received the Coronation Medal. Both she and Iris Wilkinson (Robin Hyde) were to receive this commemoration medal, and Jane's father also received one. 'Some 90,000 medals will be struck for issue as a personal souvenir from His Majesty to persons in the Crown Services and others in the United Kingdom and in other parts of the empire.'[5] Jane and Iris Wilkinson were amused at being selected to receive the award, but even more amused when they heard that D'Arcy Cresswell was peeved that he hadn't been included on the list.

Of all the news that Jane had in 1937 the best was that Robert Hale and Co. and Whitcombe and Tombs were going to reprint *The Story of a New Zealand River* the following year. The reviews of the book were all good. Frank Sargeson summed it up when he said 'It is 18 years since Miss Jane Mander's first novel *The Story of a New Zealand River* was published ... One imagines that not many New Zealand novels so far written could stand republishing after such a number of years.'[6] When she knew that Sargeson was going to review her book, Jane wrote to him and said that he didn't have to boost the book more honestly than he felt he could. She saw in it ghastly faults, and thought that she could not read it again. She said that she would have hated to review *The Story of a New Zealand River* herself, as she knew that 'its crudities would hit me in the eye now' but she then says 'I hope the old book will have a bit of luck for it has had a strange history.'[7] Whitcombe and Tombs, who were to distribute the book, were late getting it onto their shelves, and the reviews were out before the book was available. They had held it back because their sale was on; as Jane said in a resigned way, 'They have their queer ways.' Once again, she suffered from poor marketing when her book was published.

The review that delighted her the most was the one which Monte

Holcroft did for *The Press*. What impressed her was not that he said such good things about the book but that it was such a good piece of writing, she thought it a fine criticism and miles ahead of most that was seen in England at that time. In a letter to Monte Holcroft she said, 'What a beautiful job you've made of it! I'd like to think the book inspired all of it, but I can't quite believe it. Anyway as a review it entirely puts to shame the scrappy superficial stuff I send to the *Monocle*, but my head has been so tired lately that I'm no good.'[8] The Holcroft review began,

> *The Story of a New Zealand River* is one of those books that everybody knows by name. In recent years it has been spoken of as perhaps the most important New Zealand novel; but this reputation has been the result of the loyalty and admiration of a handful of discriminating readers: it has not yet gained the sudden eminence which comes when word of a good book goes round in a mysterious agitation of the collective mind. There is now every reason to believe that the delay is over, and that *The Story of a New Zealand River* will become the subject of widespread and surprised interest.[9]

There was an added bonus to this review: one of Jane's Christchurch relatives sent a copy of the review to Frank Mander, and it impressed him enormously. It put Jane in a totally different light in her father's eyes, and it was a good turn done by that relative. Her father finally began to regard Jane's work as perhaps being worthwhile; she in turn hoped that this change in his attitude toward her would mean that she would receive some money or at least be given a holiday.

Modest about her own work, Jane made the comment to John Schroder at *The Press* that the Holcroft review was that of a friend, and reiterated that maybe the review was not altogether inspired by the book. Jane was being too humble, for in another review in the magazine *Tomorrow* (3 August 1938) the critic ends the piece by stating that '*The Story of a New Zealand River* should be read by everyone who is interested in New Zealand literature.'

Although Jane was pleased with the reception of her book by people who mattered to her, she still did not receive large royalties from the sales. And underlying her pleasure at seeing the book republished was her concern and horror at the impending evil which was spreading across Europe. In contrast to her attitude to World War I, when she would argue politics with anyone who would sit near her, now in her early sixties she was upset at what she reluctantly realised was the inevitability of another war. It made her feel dislocated, and disrupted, and it played on her mind to such an extent that she found she could not settle to work on her book. She was trying to start on a book of reminiscences of her twenty years overseas, but the threat of another war made her feel that everything else was of no account.

She did start the book, but all that exists is a page entitled 'Preface to Reminiscences'. It begins,

> I don't claim to have been told more secrets than any other woman, but I do claim to have kept more secrets than most women, and those who have confided them to me may be sure they will still be kept.[10]

Then in a revealing paragraph she writes:

> I was intended to play the role of being visible in the background, as Ron Landau puts it ... I love looking on at life much more than strutting about in it. I should love parties if only I could sit in a corner, knowing everyone present, or at least who they are, and watch the comedy and the farce... I ought to have been born a rich woman, or at any rate a well to do one. I should have made if trained, quite a decent patron of the arts, and an encourager of the young, especially the talented and beautiful young. I have always been far more interested in other people's work than in my own. That is why I have been a very minor novelist and owner of most of the world's best novels by other people. In that I have been entirely frustrated. I might have made a good Beethoven player. I have large powerful rugged hands. But I had nothing but a cracked harmonium to play on till I was able to afford a piano, and then it was too late. I went to school too late to earn a scholarship. I developed too late to be blessed or destroyed by marriage. I left home and New Zealand too late to establish myself in England before the war broke out. I developed a critical sense too late, studied art too late, loved everybody too late always saw jokes too late and all because I insisted on living in a private world of my own from which I was eternally being jerked to miss the right second ...[11]

It is rare that Jane pulls aside the curtain for others to see the frustrations and disappointments she has felt, and it is a pity that there is only this tantalising fragment left from what would have been a fascinating insight into her life.

Jane's daily life was far removed from her days in London and New York, and she was further and further divorced from friends and events which had been the mainstay of her life when she had lived there. She felt her isolation. She was still burdened with caring for her family, and none of the promises (bribes) made back in 1932 had come to fruition. In 1941 there was little time for any of her own work, as once again her loved sister-in-law was ill and for most of the year Jane was her nurse. When at the end of the year she died, Jane's brother Bert collapsed and it then fell to Jane to care for him during his illness. It is not surprising that by the time she had nursed him to health, she was herself ill. She had conjunctivitis in her right eye which no matter what treatment it was given continued plaguing her for about eight months; she could neither read nor write during that time, and her frustration grew greater daily. Finally, her father had a stroke and became bedridden; it took Jane a long time to find a nurse who would come and look after her father, and until one was found she nursed him herself. Added to all this was the concern in Auckland of a Japanese invasion: each house had to have blackouts, and each day there were sirens practising for the 'real thing'. It is no wonder that Jane was staggering under the load.

At last she found someone to care for her father. Muriel was everything anyone could hope for in a nurse, she was quick and efficient, but kind too, and at last Jane felt she could plan to have a holiday. By the time the nurse had settled in and there had been the usual Christmas upheavals with providing a festive season for the rest of the family, it was April 1942 before Jane managed to get away for a rest. She was exhausted and referred to herself as having a 'tired heart'.[12] As usual she went north to camp, to rest, to read and to walk along the beaches around Whangarei Harbour. It was as well that she had no premonition of the upheaval which was to greet her when she returned home to Auckland.

While Jane had been recuperating in the north her brother Bert, who had been a widower for the past six months fell 'violently in love' (Jane's words) with Muriel. Muriel had promised Jane that she would stay 'to see the old man out', but now Bert wanted to marry her and spirit her away, leaving Jane with the business of looking after her father and also looking for a new nurse. It was an utter bombshell for Jane.

Finally they all reached a compromise. Muriel agreed to stand by Jane and help find a new nurse. She and Bert would marry later in the year and move into 10 Keith Avenue; they would have the two large rooms, which had been Jane's, and they would take over the running of the house. Jane would move all her books and belongings into two smaller rooms. The change-over was a 'horrid mess'[13] for her, but it was the best that could be sorted out.

The compromise started to fall apart when Bert and Muriel decided they couldn't wait until the end of the year to marry and so brought the date forward to 15 August. Just before the wedding Frank Mander suffered a mild stroke, but then seemed to rally. The wedding went ahead and Bert and Muriel went off to a beach cottage for their honeymoon.

Jane was left to find a nurse for her father and to run the household. Her father then suffered another stroke which left him with a paralysed throat. Jane eventually managed to get nursing care, but it was fragmented;

at one stage there were three different nurses coming at three different times during the day. Frank Mander died on 27 August 1942, nearly 10 years after Jane's return to New Zealand.

Not surprisingly, after her father's funeral Jane collapsed and had to go to bed indefinitely with what she called her 'tired heart'. She wrote to Monte Holcroft that if she were not so seedy she would be thrilled that she was free at last – 'No one knows what a horror the last four years have been for me'.[14]

After all the promises he made of giving money to Jane when he died, Frank Mander's will is odd. He gave to his two daughters Annie and Amy and his son Bert three thousand pounds outright. Jane shared the residue of the estate with her three sisters and her brother. The estate came to twenty-two thousand pounds; by the time it was divided equally between the five of them, Jane would have received about four thousand three hundred pounds. Not a huge sum, considering the work she had done. The bribe had worked in favour of Frank Mander. His only unmarried daughter who was capable of caring for him had come home and fulfilled her familial obligations; she had come on false promises, she had stayed under duress, and now with at last the freedom to take up her life as she would wish, he had short-changed her and she was too ill.

The house in Keith Avenue in Remuera was sold in 1943, about six months after Frank Mander's death, and Jane moved to a small apartment at 7 Waimea Lane, off Victoria Avenue in Remuera. Those who visited her at that apartment were delighted by the beauty with which she surrounded herself. Paintings, china, rugs and of course books. Her eyesight was now weak and she could not continue with the amount of reading and reviewing she had been doing, but she had a huge collection of records and would sit and listen with enjoyment to the music she loved. Those who visited her at Waimea Lane remember a household which was welcoming and well run. She maintained her forthright opinions, and maybe as a legacy from her father's days of driving erratically around Remuera, she was terrified of speed in a car. Olive de Malmanche, who was her neighbour and good friend, remembers taking Jane for a Sunday drive; Jane sat in the back seat and would tell them, loudly, they were going far too fast as soon as they got over a speed of forty miles per hour.

For three years Jane stayed in her apartment enjoying the feast of friends, without the constraints of her irascible father. As well as her poor eyesight, the war had affected her ability to work: she became absorbed by 'the world of contemporary events, the colossal disasters and problems and constructive feats and magnificent endurance and spiritual strength, but what is to come of it all'.[15] She was amazed at people who were still able to write what she referred to as 'silly fiction' and even more amazed at the number of people who were reading it. She now had to be careful not to over-exert herself, for if she did she then had to return to bed. After being so involved with so many of the writers in Auckland she now saw few of them. She comments to Monte Holcroft that 'Sargesson[sic] I think, has got as far as he can with his particular gift. Fairburn is smothered in the inanities of IZB programme making (there's a tragedy) and R.A.K. Mason writes nothing save for *The People's Voice* and flits mysteriously from one pathetic shack to another.'[16]

When the war ended and the atomic bomb was dropped on Nagasaki and Hiroshima, Jane was distraught. Always interested in what was happening internationally, she was appalled that something as terrible as an atomic bomb could have been made and used to kill humans. She became depressed and could not see what would save what she referred to as Western civilisation. She thought constantly about the world's mess, and became very despondent when she met people who did not think about the world situation at all and expected things to go on comfortably in New Zealand for their children and their grandchildren. Her consolation, somewhat barren, was that she thought she would not live long enough to witness an atomic war.

Jane finally had to accept that her health was precarious. It was agreed that it would be a wise move to go back to Whangarei to live. There she would be close to her young sister and to her brother. Her cousin Horace Kerr set about building her an attractive flat in Lovatt's Crescent, but before she could move to Whangarei she had a slight stroke, and was in hospital and a rest home for three months. The family had to finish her packing and arrange for all her furniture and books to be sent to Whangarei. It was Christmas 1946 before she was able to write to any of her friends, and her letter to the Holcrofts is not so much about her difficulties, as about how glad she was that Monte Holcroft had won the Hubert Church award for the second time. She was particularly pleased that he had beaten J.C. Reid, who had always been as Jane put it 'very sniffy about my novels'. She said that she was human enough to be annoyed about it, and although she didn't overrate her own work she felt he could have been kinder to *The Story of a New Zealand River.*

The house that the Kerrs built for Jane delighted her; it was roomy and on one level and she set about once more creating a beautiful and memorable surrounding. Unfortunately before she could begin to enjoy her new life in her new home she had another stroke and was again confined to bed.

On 26 September 1948 Jane wrote her last letter to Monte Holcroft, still in her bold strong handwriting:

Dear Monte

Have been meaning to write to say how I enjoyed your fine review in the Listener *of John Mulgan's* Report on Experience *and to ask how you are getting on since you left the* Southland Times – *very well, I see now, since you are off to Paris and UNESCO. What a fine experience that will be! I'm very pleased. You won't have time to write before you go, but do get Ray to write and tell me the news. You will be sending articles to N.Z. papers I presume, and shall hope to see some of them. The* Herald, *I feel sure, would take a series. I'm emerging slowly from my very serious illness and hope by another year to be really well again. Best wishes for your voyage and good luck with all it will mean.*

Ever your old friend Jane.

Despite her hopes for better health by the following year this was not to be, and the fighting spark of this forthright, fascinating woman was overcome.

Jane Mander died in Whangarei on 20 December 1949.

CHAPTER FIFTEEN

≈

If Aunt Jane had been alive today she would have knee-capped Jane Campion.[1]

Judy Beetham, Jane Mander's great niece

The Story of A New Zealand River has had an interesting life. Ever since its gestation period, and the long wait for its birth in 1920, it has been a book which has been praised, ignored, denigrated, and mishandled. The first edition was poorly printed; paper was in short supply, and it was published in a period before publishers realised the importance of a good cover; later it was badly marketed. After its reprint in 1938, the book dropped from sight.

In 1960 a new edition of the book was published by Whitcoulls, and this was reprinted in 1973, 1974 and 1975. These later editions had an introduction by Dr Dorothea Turner, who had published a biography of Jane Mander in 1972. Dr Turner's introduction begins, 'Books are easily prevented but quite hard to kill once they are in print. They lie around in obscure places like spores, ready to proliferate when the climate changes.'

The climate for New Zealand books had begun to change, and in the 1960s a new feeling of identity started to permeate New Zealand. With the world-wide move towards liberation from old mores, there was a movement in the country away from being the colonial outpost of Great Britain. Picture theatres still commenced each session with a picture of the Monarch while 'God Save the Queen' was played, but fewer movie fans stood to attention, as had been the custom in the past. This growing silent protest was a public statement of New Zealanders wanting their own identity. Droves of young people still travelled overseas for the great OE, but just as many returned, tugged home by the memories of freedom from class distinction, and of the beauty of their home country and its weather.

In 1960 it was not only Jane's book that was re-published. John Mulgan's *Man Alone* was back on the shop shelves, and so were Robyn Hyde's *Check to Your King* and Alan Mulgan's *Spur of Morning.* New Zealanders started to ask 'Who are we?' Answers were sought and sometimes found in the literature of the country; as with Jane Mander, foreign travel had given many of these people some perspective in viewing their own land.

In 1994, Godwit Press republished *The Story of A New Zealand River*. Once again Dorothea Turner's introduction was included, this time as an afterword. This edition came close on the heels of a masters paper introduced in the English Department at the University of Auckland in 1993. The paper was called Australian and New Zealand Women Writers and included a study of the novel.

The Story of a New Zealand River is set on one of the trailing tidal fingers of the Kaipara River at Oruawhero. The opening chapter begins with an expletive, 'Damnation'. David Bruce, who is to take the boss's wife and family up the river to their new home, is anxious to get going, as the tide is running out fast. The boat is packed with boxes and furniture and at last Alice Roland and her three children arrive. David Bruce is struck with the beauty and dignity of Alice, but she sees him only as a servant. It is left to her daughter Asia to show any friendliness towards him. And it is Asia who is immediately beguiled by the scenery around her and the excitement of being on the river. Alice tries to look as divorced as possible from the whole adventure, which is so foreign to everything she has so far known. With her head down, she endeavours to ignore her surroundings and appears unrelated to anything other than her piano.

> Then Alice stood up. The only thing that seemed to belong to her, in that incongruous setting of boxes and mattresses and common furniture, was a piano which was packed in a heavy case.[2]

Alice's journey, we learn later in the story, begins long before the opening chapters. She has been brought up in an English Victorian household where there is no female influence. Her puritanical father forbids any outside contact. She admits her emotional education is limited to reading 'silly romances' and she readily falls in love with an older man. In defiance of her father she continues the romance, and the result is her pregnancy. The outcome of this defiance of male authority is that she is cast out of the family. The child's father disappears, and Alice with some help from a brother goes to Australia to have the baby. From Australia she moves to New Zealand, in order to gain some form of respectability by posing as a widow who will teach the piano.

Alice with a child is in New Zealand without any traditional male support. Tom Roland comes upon her when she has just lost her purse. She is destitute, he looked kind, and so she agrees to marry him.

Alice begins her journey up the river, to an isolated settlement going to a man she doesn't love, to a place she doesn't know, with children, and with the fear that there will be other children to come. She has come from a sheltered background, and is ill-equipped for frontier life, clinging like a barnacle to the only two sure things she has: her narrow-minded moral outlook, and her piano.

David Bruce falls in love with Alice, and Alice is terrified of the feelings that she has for him. Her prime concern is to maintain her dignity, to bring up her family in a strict fashion, and be a dutiful wife. It is a very long time before she admits to herself that she is able to love in a passionate and fulfilling way. She must kill the impulse even to think of him. But she was secretly afraid of her impulses.

> She could not understand why anyone who hated them as much as she did should have them so violently. She had been taught and she still believed that impulses were monstrous inventions of evil to be fought and suppressed. Her own experience had already taught her their terrible results.[3]

Her great release from the internalising of emotions and subduing of natural reactions to sexual excitement is to play the piano. The music flows out across the night as a release from all the tension and misery. It is through her daughter Asia's influence that she gradually starts to shed the puritanical carapace she created for herself.

'I wish you would like Mr. Bruce. I think he's lovely.'[4] Asia says ingenuously to her mother. Where Asia can love someone openly and happily, that is dangerous ground for Alice. She has married out of need and gratitude and for protection, and by sealing off her emotions she can continue to do her duty as she sees it should be done:

> After all it was simple. Duty always was when you faced it clearly. She realised that above all things she wanted peace. She thought of her compensations. She had Mrs. Brayton and her children; she had her music and her books.[5]

David Bruce is a continual presence. He is there to soothe her fears when her husband Tom Roland leaves her alone to go off searching for more bush to cut. He is there when she is ill, and when she gives birth, and when the consequences of that birth leave her bedridden.

Alice has great difficulty in expressing her emotions. Often her mute acceptance of what is happening around her is an irritation to the reader. Why can't this woman stop internalising and allow herself to speak out? Why can't she relax and enjoy her emotions, despite the pain it may bring? The opinion of many readers is that the woman needs a good shake. But Mander worked at building up the tension between how Alice sees herself, how she 'should behave', and how she truly feels.

It is a huge relief to the reader when Alice finally makes the decision that whether there is a God or not she has the right to have David Bruce as her friend. Her rugged introspective journey is moving into calmer waters. Throughout the story, Asia is the balance to Alice. Where Alice stumbles, Asia rushes to embrace the world to experience and enjoy life, to never be bound by rules which curb the intellect or the passion. Asia says 'Mother has taught me one great lesson. I'm done with misery. I shall have nothing more to do with it as long as I live. I shall train my mind to ignore it.'[6]

The triangle of the woman, the husband and the attractive 'other' man is not a new plot, but Jane Mander interweaves the ebb and flow of the river with the ebb and flow of Alice's realisation of her self. It seems at times a tortuous journey. When she does find her voice and can state her needs and wants, the most surprised person is her daughter Asia:

> 'Mother, what has happened to you?' she asked, trying to steady her voice. 'To me?' Alice looked at her and away again. 'Why nothing. I just see things differently.'[7]

The novel concludes with Alice a widow, as Tom Roland has had an accident in the bush and is killed. She and David Bruce finally come together, and move away from the mill town to make a new life in Auckland. Alice's journey has been completed.

Why is this book so durable?

Joan Stevens wrote that '*The Story of a New Zealand River* stands out from those barren years 1900-1930 as an example of a novel which is really *about* something which is really attempting to interpret life.'[8] It is a story about people who could be a neighbour or a friend or a relative. It is a story about a coming to terms with oneself, and a story about marriage in a colonial setting. It does not glorify the colonial woman – Alice does not fit the romanticised picture of the steadfast frontier woman who can turn her hand to anything.

The description of the bush and the felling of the great kauri is a record of what the great forests of the north once were. But apart from documentary aspects of the book, the story tries to present a situation which shows that women were entitled to have sexual feelings. Before this novel most writers in New Zealand ignored the sexuality of women, it was a topic that was given the airbrush treatment. Women had babies seemingly by immaculate conception, and childbirth was borne with great fortitude, and according to the novelists regarded as a wonderful gift from God. Jane Mander wanted to write about what she saw were real concerns for women in remote areas: the fear of a pregnancy, and the terrors of childbirth. She also wrote of the need for women to be able to use contraception. She tried to portray women as individuals, not as goddesses. In *The Story of a New Zealand River* it is Asia, the new woman, who promotes the importance of contraception. For Alice, it is something that cannot be countenanced. She still takes the puritanical stance of regarding contraception as something for prostitutes.

In writing about such topics, Jane Mander was trying to achieve a realism in human relationships, using as a backdrop the hard rawness of life in a timber milling settlement. Despite her loathing for films, it is a story which would make a great film.

In 1985 John Maynard and Brigid Ikin bought the film rights to the book, from Jane's nephew Rangi Cross through the literary agent Ray Richards. Both Ikin and Maynard were producers with a solid background in film making. John Maynard had amongst other work produced *The Navigator*, and Brigid Ikin had worked with Jane Campion as the producer on the film of Janet Frame's life, *Angel at my Table*.

With assistance from the New Zealand Film Commission of $102,000, Ikin and Maynard worked for the next five years on the script for a film which they were calling 'The River'. Several writers worked on the script and there were approximately nine drafts.

According to Bob Harvey, who was deputy chairman of the New Zealand Film Commission at the time, *The River* was a lovely story with excellent producers, and they wanted Jane Campion to be the director. However, Jane Campion had seen the script and had not been impressed. She said there would have to be substantial changes to it before she would be interested.

Meanwhile the New Zealand Film Commission, still under the impression that Jane Campion would be directing *The River*, saw a clip from the film *Broadcast News* in which Holly Hunter was the lead. It was suggested that she would be a possibility for the role of Alice in *The River*. It had already been suggested that Sam Neill play the part of David Bruce.

The surprise news for the New Zealand Film Commission was that Jane Campion was not available to work on *The River*. She was now wholly involved in her own film, which was being funded by a French company Ciby 2000 and the Australian Film Commission, with Holly Hunter and Sam Neill in leading roles. While Ikin and Maynard were working on their film, Jane Campion had begun work on a film of her own, initially called 'The Piano Player'.

The filmscript of *The River* begins in the early morning. A punt is sitting in the river laden with trunks and crates and a tarpaulin which covered a piano has been removed. Two men are looking at it in astonishment when Alice Roland arrives. She makes the statement that the piano must go, and that if the piano doesn't go then neither does she. The importance to Alice of the piano is established.

Jane Campion's 'The Piano Player' was eventually released as *The Piano*. The film begins with the unloading of a piano onto a beach through the surf. The importance of the piano to Ada is immediately made clear when she insists that it is carried through the bush to the house, which is finally achieved through the efforts of Baines, not her husband.

It is quite common for projects for films to be developed contemporaneously. For example, when another New Zealand film, *Heavenly Creatures*, was being developed there were other film-makers interested in the story of the Parker-Hulme murder. But Jane Campion knew that her good friends were already working on *The River*, so why set up a project that was so similar that it caused such rancour amongst so many people? Was it arrogance or ego, or was it simply that she thought the film she was making was so different from *The River* that it didn't matter? These questions will probably never be answered.

A veil of silence covers those who were involved.

Rangi Cross, Jane Mander's nephew, said that because of legal constraints he could not talk about any aspect of what went on, apart from confirming the sale of the original film rights to John Maynard and Brigid Ikin in 1985. He also said that he would never go and see the 'damn film'[9] (meaning *The Piano*).

Ray Richards, Jane Mander's literary executor, suggested that I contact John Maynard directly, and gave me an address from which I received no reply. In a TV2 20/20 documentary Richards had said that his lips were sealed and that 'the whole thing had been so subtle he wouldn't even attempt to explain the superficialities of it.'[10]

In a polite note Judith McCann, who had been executive director of the New Zealand Film Commission at the time, writes 'I regard myself as continuing to be bound by confidentiality in respect of any matter involving the NZFC's business during that period.'

In a conversation with Bob Harvey,[11] he said that Jane Campion and Brigid Ikin went to Cannes together to market *Angel at My Table*. They had been good friends before making the Frame film and Jane Campion was godmother to Ikin and Maynard's son. Miramax were keen to distribute *Angel at my Table* and maybe it was at this time that Jane Campion was asked if she had any other project in mind. The question is, did Jane Campion discuss a film about a woman and a piano on a river? There is no way this can be answered because it is speculation.

Back in New Zealand the Film Commission, with their investment in *The River*, were waiting for the film to get under way. Suddenly there were letters and faxes flying between the Hibiscus Films project and Jan Chapman Productions, the producer of *The Piano*.[12]

According to the TV2 20/20 programme, it seemed that in order to have the pre-production money for *The Piano* it was necessary for Maynard and Ikin to sign a release of the film rights, and to withdraw allegations that the Campion film breached copyright and obligations of confidence. Perhaps the friendship was becoming strained, because no release was signed, and there were threats of a court action. The New Zealand Film Commission was asked to waive the $102,000 they had invested in *The River*. If the release was signed, the Film Commission would get its money back. The New Zealand Film Commission refused.

There was no court case and maybe it was agreed that legal action would benefit no one, least of all the film industry.

The New Zealand Film Commission had wanted Jane Campion to acknowledge that the story of *The Piano* was inspired by *The Story of a New Zealand River*. She would not agree to this. Strangely, Campion offered the New Zealand Film Commission a screen credit which they turned down. Jane Campion has said that the inspiration for her film came from many sources; that is often the way with any art. She said that she had read about twenty books which gave her ideas for the film, and that the book which influenced her the most was *Wuthering Heights*, a book well and truly out of copyright.

Those who knew The *Story of a New Zealand River* well immediately saw similarities between the book and the film *The Piano*.

Both book and film have a pioneering New Zealand background.

In the book the woman is called Alice. In the film the woman is Ada. Both have precocious young daughters. Both arrive in New Zealand with a child and marry here. Neither Alice nor Ada loves her husband. Both fall in love with another man, and central to the expression of their emotions is the piano. Each woman discovers her own sexuality through the love of a man other than her husband.

The book begins with a punt being loaded with furniture and a piano to go on a trip up a river. The film begins with boxes and a piano being unloaded through the surf onto a beach. Both Alice and Ada have to endure the isolation and roughness of bush life. Jane Mander describes clearly the type of house and environment that Alice lived in, which was ill-favoured and graceless. Jane Campion emphasises the isolation, with scenes of Ada and Flora dragging their long skirts through deep mud in dripping bush.

Both women allow their emotions to flow out through their piano. In *The Piano* the music is Ada's own, an escape into her own world. In the book the music is Beethoven, which Alice makes her own in order to escape her surroundings:

Alice played to a world of her own, to something in herself that had no other means of expression. She played with delicacy and with passion, with unerring feeling for balance, for light and shade.[13]

At the end of *The Piano*, Ada goes with George Baines, her lover, to make a life together away from the bush. At the end of *The Story of a New Zealand River*, Alice goes with David Bruce, her lover, to make a life together away from the bush.

The Campion film introduced a Maori element, which Jane Mander never used in her story. In the film it emphasised the aloneness of Baines, an intelligent man from nowhere looking for a place. Although there is no Maori influence in *The Story of a New Zealand River*, David Bruce was also someone from nowhere, a doctor with no practice and a secret binge drinker, not quite a remittance man but another intelligent man searching for his place.

In the film, Ada's husband Stewart, is more interested in acquiring land than bothering with his wife. Likewise in Mander's book, Tom Roland is keen to acquire land and trees to cut. Neither Stewart nor Roland shows any inclination to understand his wife.

With the many similarities between the film *The Piano* and the book *The Story of a New Zealand River*, it would seem that Jane Mander should at least have been acknowledged for supplying the basic idea for the film. Was it that there were problems as to who had the film rights to the Jane Mander book, which meant that Jane Campion could not legally say that she had used the book as a basis for her film? Was it that Jane Campion honestly didn't see any of the similarities between her work and the book once she began work on the film?

Jane Campion has remarked that it is a New Zealand attitude that if someone does well they must have cheated. That has been said before, and there may be a kernel of truth in the allegation. Cutting people who are successful down to size – the 'Tall Poppy Syndrome' is as well known in New Zealand as it is in Australia, where the term was coined.

Vernon Knowles wrote,

Ill luck of different kinds – but always virulent in quality – has attacked each one of her books – from the first one, *The Story of a New Zealand River*, published in war time, when labour was scarce, and materials were as exorbitant in price as they were poor in value; to the last one, *Pins and Pinnacles...* Illnesses and strikes, wretched publicity and inappropriate publishing dates; these have all been her portion from time to time, book by book; and her name is not so well known as it should be. As the most distinguished woman writer that New Zealand has produced, she comes second only to Katherine Mansfield.[14]

Had she been alive, Jane Mander would have re-emphasised her comment to Monte Holcroft, 'What a trial it is to be a writer.'[15]

FINIS

Jane Mander's grave can be found at the Maunu Cemetery in Whangarei. She is the only Mander listed in the records of that cemetery. Her headstone says simply:

Mary Jane Mander 20 December 1949

Please don't turn me into a ghost. I should be the most uneasy spirit you have ever known. But if you do, let me have a cemetery all to myself. I insist on it. I will not be put with the relatives.

Jane Mander, *The Strange Attraction*, p. 294

Acknowledgements

≈

Many people have helped me with this book. Not least my husband Gavin who has lived with this 'other woman' in our lives for over three years. It was he who paid for me to visit New York and London as part of the research. To him my heartfelt thanks and love.

My daughter Louise has cheerfully helped with research, and I thank her most sincerely.

Librarians often get a bad press, but in every case librarians where I have researched material have been professional, helpful, kind, and encouraging. Thanks to: Alexander Turnbull Library, Auckland City Central Library, Barnard College Archives, Devonport Public Library, National Archives, New South Wales State Library (Mitchell Library), New York City Public Library, Wellington General Assembly Library, Wellington Maritime Museum Library, Whangarei Public Library, and the University of Auckland Library.

The Sargeson Trust allowed me to have access to the Sargeson papers, held at the Alexander Turnbull Library.

The *Northern Advocate* newspaper, the Whangarei Museum, and The Kauri Museum, Matakohe, have all helped with finding and printing photographs. I am indebted to the people who organised for this to be done.

The following people gave me the gift of their time in order to help with the research: Amanda and John Banks, Judy Beetham, Mandy Brown, Monica Carolan, Geoff Chapple, Rangi Cross, Olive de Malmanche, Rae Hammer, Bob Harvey, Ron and Kaye Holloway, Allan and Geraldine Kerr, John and Colleen Kerr, Michele Leggott, Jane Lowenthal, Helen and Alwyn O'Connor, Mary Paul, Robyn Sievwright, Peter Simpson, and Len Vivian.

I am enormously grateful to Wendy Harrex, managing editor at the University of Otago Press. Not only has she gently steered me through the process of getting a book published, but she has also been the valuable editor of this work.

Finally I would like to thank the late Dr Dorothea Turner for her generosity in letting me look at all the material she had gathered for her own research on Jane Mander. In particular Dr Turner allowed me the exclusive use of letters which Jane had written home to her sister. Copies of these are now with the rest of Jane Mander's papers in the Auckland Central City Library. Dr Turner's encouragement to me for the book was something I will always value. My regret is that it wasn't completed before she died.

RAE McGREGOR
Mangawhai, May 1998

NOTES

≈

Preface

[1] May Knight, 'Jane Mander Loved Everything Blue', *Auckland Star*, 22 December 1949, p. 6 [NZMS 535 APL].

Chapter One

[1] Andrew Gurr, *Writers in Exile: The Identity of Home in Modern Literature* (Brighton, Sussex: 1981), p. 17.

[2] Letter to Mrs Cross (Tommy), dated 'London 28 August 1912'. Private collection.

[3] Margaret Lewis, *Ngaio Marsh: A Life* (Wellington: Bridget Williams Books Ltd, 1991), p. 38.

[4] Letter to Mrs Cross (Tommy), 28 August 1912. Private collection.

Chapter Two

[1] Personal letter to Rae McGregor from M.B. Carolan, great grand-daughter of Sarah Ann Mander, 11 November 1996.

[2] Dorothea Turner, *Jane Mander* (New York: Twayne Publishers Inc., 1972), p. 18.

[3] 'Some Random Recollections from the 1930s' by Warwick Lawrence. Written on my request, 1995.

[4] Freda Sternberg, 'Jane Mander', *The Bookman,* March 1924, p. 296 [NZMS 535 APL].

[5] Freda Sternberg, 'Tall Houses Instead of Tall Trees', *The Home*, 1932(?) [NZMS 535 APL].

[6] Jane Mander, 'My Life in Two Worlds', *Daily Chronicle*, 28 October 1928 [NZMS 535 APL].

[7] Jane Mander, *The Story of a New Zealand River* (New York: John Lane, London: John Lane, The Bodley Head 1920, reprinted Christchurch: Whitcombe & Tombs 1938; Christchurch: Whitcombe & Tombs, London: Robert Hale, 1960; Christchurch: Whitcombe & Tombs, 1973, reprinted 1974, 1975; Auckland: Godwit Press, 1994), p. 15. All quotations are from the 1975 reprint.

[8] A.H. Reed, *The Kauri*, Wellington: A.H. & A.W. Reed, 1967, p. 6.

[9] *Ibid.*, p. 5.

[10] *Ibid.*, p. 6.

[11] *Ibid.*, p. 7.

[12] Jane Mander, *The Story of a New Zealand River,* p. 39.

[13] *Ibid.*, p. 44.

[14] Jane Mander, 'My Life in Two Worlds,' *Daily Chronicle*, 28 October 1929 [NZMS 535 APL].

15 A.H. Reed, *The Gumdiggers* (Wellington: A.H. & A.W. Reed, 1972), p. 18.

16 Jane Mander, *Allen Adair* (Auckland: Auckland University Press, 1971), p. 42.

Chapter Three

1 Sir Henry Brett and Henry Hook, *The Albertlanders: Brave Pioneers of the '60s*, (Auckland: Brett Publishing Co., 1927; Christchurch: Capper Press, reprint 1979), p. 18.

2 'W' for Worker, Watson, and White,'E' for Edger, 'L' for Lester 'S' for Simpson, Scott, Stark and Stuart, 'F' for Foster, 'O' for Oldfield, 'R' for Rushbrook, Ramsbottom, Rishworth, and 'D' for Dibble.

3 Elaine Zimmerman (compiler), *Wellsford and District Schools Centennial Booklet, 1875–1975*, p. 32.

4 *Ibid.*, p. 33.

5 *Ibid.*, p. 8.

6 *Ibid.*, p. 6.

7 R.T.V. Linnell, *Centennial of Kaiwaka: Rautau O Kaiwaka 1859–1959*, Commemorative Booklet & Souvenir Programme (Wellsford: Campbell Press, 1959), p. 8.

8 Jane Mander, *The Passionate Puritan* (London: John Lane, The Bodley Head, 1921, New York: John Lane, 1922), p. 22.

9 From *Recollections of Jane Mander*, by J.J.M. Mitchell [NZMS 535 APL]

10 *Ibid.*

11 John T. Diamond and Bruce W. Hayward, *Waitakere Kauri: A Pictorial History of the Kauri Timber Industry in the Waitakere Ranges, West Auckland* (Auckland: Lodestar Press, 1980), p. 24.

12 Personal conversation with Mrs Olive de Malmanche, 1994.

13 Bill Haigh, *Foote Prints Among the Kauri* (Whangarei: Bill Haigh, n.d.), p. 104.

Chapter Four

1 Dorothea Turner, *Jane Mander*, p. 22.

2 *Cyclopaedia of New Zealand: Auckland* (Christchurch: 1902 ed.), p. 421.

3 Letter to Johannes Andersen, 18 November 1935 [ATL].

4 'Jane Mander in Whangarei', by Nancy Pickmere [NZMS 535 APL].

5 Conversation with Nancy Pickmere, Kerikeri, 1995.

6 Jane Mander, 'A Stray Woman', *New Zealand Illustrated Magazine*, March 1902, p. 444 [NZMS 535 APL].

7 Pat Lawlor said of Frank Morton, 'It was Morton and not Baeyertz who made *The Triad*, and when Morton died (1923) *The Triad* virtually died.' *Confessions of a Journalist*, (Wellington: Whitcombe & Tombs Ltd, 1935), p. 236.

Chapter Five

1 *Grenfell Vedette*, 11 January 1899. Quoted in the Hon Mr Justice Herbert Vere Evatt, *Australian Labour Leader: The Story of W.A. Holman and the Labour Movement* (Sydney: Angus and Robertson Ltd, 1940), p. 138.

2   *Australian Labour Leader: The Story of W.A. Holman and the Labour Movement*, p. 18.

3   Manda Lloyd [Jane Mander], 'A Woman's View', *The Maoriland Worker*, 12 July 1911, p. 5 [University of Auckland Library].

4   Manda Lloyd [Jane Mander], 'The Children's Court, The Problem of the Neglected and the Unwanted Child', *The Maoriland Worker*, 24 November 1911, p. 7 [NZMS 535 APL].

5   *Ibid.*

6   *Ibid.*

Chapter Six

1   'Eighteen Story Skyscraper to Replace Old Cotton Exchange', *New York Times*, 1 September 1912, p. 9 [New York Library].

2   Dorothea Turner, *Jane Mander* (University of Texas: Twayne & Co Publishers Ltd, 1972), p. 25 [Records in the School of Journalism Library, Columbia University].

3   *Ibid*, p. 25.

4   Jane Mander, 'New Zealand Novels – The Struggle Against Environment', *The Press*, 15 December 1934 [NZMS 535 APL]. Other articles in the series were: 'Short Stories – Scope for Dominion Writers' (1 December) and 'New Zealand Novels – Character, Action, and Scene' (8 December).

5   Horace Coon, *Columbia Collossus on the Hudson* (New York: E.P. Dutton & Company Inc, 1947), p. 203.

6   Letter to Mrs Cross (Tommy), '1 December 1913 New York 10.30 a.m'. Private collection.

7   Jane Mander, 'Living Conditions for Women in New York and London'. Talk given to the YWCA, Auckland, 1932 [NZMS 535 APL].

8   *Ibid.*

9   Letter to Mrs Cross (Tommy), 1 December 1913. Private collection.

10   Dorothea Turner, *Jane Mander*, p. 27.

11   Jane Mander, *The Besieging City* (London: Hutchinson & Co Publishers Ltd, 1926), p. 153.

12   Letter to Mrs Cross (Tommy), 1 December 1913. Private collection.

13   Jane Mander, *The Besieging City*, p. 28.

14   Letter to Mrs Cross (Tommy), 20 August 1913(?). Private collection.

Chapter Seven

1   Mary Gray Peck, *Carrie Chapman Catt: A Biography.* (New York: H.W. Wilson Company, 1944), p. 229.

2   Letter to Mrs Cross (Tommy), 15 November 1914. Private collection.

3   Talk given to the Lyceum Club, 8 June 1933 [NZMS 535 APL].

4   Mary Gray Peck, *Carrie Chapman Catt – A Biography*, p. 220.

5   Letter to Mrs Cross (Tommy), 1 September 1915. Private collection.

6   *Ibid.*

7   Personal conversation with Rangi Cross, 1995.

8   Letter to Mrs Cross (Tommy), 3 June 1915. Private collection.

9   'Working During Vacation – Teachers at Trenton Falls', *Utica Daily Press,* 29 July 1915 [NZMS 535 APL].
10   Letter to Mrs Cross (Tommy), 1 September 1915. Private collection.
11   Mary Gray Peck, *Carrie Chapman Catt – A Biography,* pp. 229-230.
12   Lisa A. Callahan, 'Sing Sing Prison', in Marilyn D. McShane and Frank P. Williams III (eds), *Encyclopaedia of American Prisons* (New York: Garland Publishing Inc., 1996), pp. 443-6.
13   Rudolph W. Chamberlain, *There is No Truce: A Life of Thomas Mott Osborne* (Freeport, New York: 1935), p. 295.
14   'Convicts Cheer Return of "Tom Brown" from Society Resorts', *New York Times,* 31 August 1915 [New York Public Library].
15   Letter to Mrs Cross (Tommy), 1 September 1915. Private collection.
16   Editorial, *New Republic: A Journal of Opinion,* Volume IV, 7 August 1915, p. 2 [NZMS 535 APL].

Chapter Eight
1   Jane Mander, *The Besieging City,* p. 11.
2   'Living Conditions for Women in New York and London'. Talk given to the YWCA, 1932 [NZMS 535 APL].
3   Manuscript of a talk for radio given in 1932 [NZMS 535 APL].
4   *Ibid.*
5   Letter to John A. Lee, 6 May 1936 [NZMS 441/15 APL].
6   Jane Mander, *The Story of a New Zealand River,* p. 175.
7   Letter to Mrs Cross (Tommy), 28 August 1912. Private collection.
8   Letter to Mrs Cross (Tommy), 10 April 1917. Private collection.
9   *Ibid.*
10   *Ibid.*
11   Jane Mander, *The Besieging City,* p. 36.
12   Personal conversation with Olive de Malmanche, 1994.
13   Jane Mander, *The Story of a New Zealand River,* p. 169.
14   Jane Mander, *The Besieging City,* pp. 37, 38.
15   'A Brief Biography'. Sent to Johannes Andersen, 3 November 1935 [Ms papers 0148 Folder 029/10 ATL].
16   Letter to Mrs Cross (Tommy), 30 December 1918. Private collection.
17   Letter to Mrs Cross (Tommy), 12 November 1918. Private collection.

Chapter Nine
1   Freda Sternberg, 'Tall Houses Instead of Tall Trees', *The Home,* 1932(?) [NZMS 535 APL].
2   Letter to John A. Lee, 6 May 1936 [APL NZMS 441/15].
3   Letter to Johannes Andersen, 18 November 1935 [Ms Papers 1186-16 ATL].
4   Letter to Frank Sargeson, dated 'Sunday', probably 1938 from internal evidence [Sargeson Papers ATL].
5   Letter to John A. Lee, 31 October 1936 [NZMS 441/15 APL].

6   Letter from Alan E. Mulgan to *The London Mercury*, undated [NZMS 535 APL].
7   Andrew Gurr, *Writers in Exile: The Identity of Home in Modern Literature*, p. 18.
8   Dorothea Turner, *Jane Mander*, p. 29.

Chapter Ten

1   Date and place of publication of this article has not yet been located by the author.
2   Jane Mander, 'On Making Good – Colonials in London – Mr Punch's Advice Stressed', *Sun* (Christchurch), 4 December 1924 [NZMS 535 APL].
3   Jane Mander, 'Well Known People I Have Met Abroad'. Talk given to the Lyceum Club, Auckland, 8 June 1933 [NZMS 535 APL].
4   Jane Mander, 'On Making Good – Colonials in London'.
5   Jane Mander, 'Flats for Single Women', *Time and Tide*, 25 April 1924, pp. 403, 404 [NZMS 535 APL].
6   *Ibid.*
7   Jane Mander, 'Reading Manuscripts for a Publisher', *Samoa Times*, 7 November 1924 [NZMS 535 APL].
8   Jane Mander, 'A London Letter: New Zealand Novelist Writes of Art and Famous Men', *Sun* (Auckland), 26 March 1927.
9   Jane Mander, 'On Making Good – Colonials in London'.
10 Jane Mander, 'Sir Beelzebub and his Syllabub – An Evening with the Moderns', *Sun* (Christchurch), 12 June 1926 [NZMS 535 APL].
11 Jane Mander, 'La Vie de Bohème', *Sun* (Christchurch), 28 November 1925, p. 12 [NZMS 535 APL].
12 Letter from A.G. Stephens, *The Bookfellow*, Sydney, Australia, 14 June 1923 [NZMS 535 APL].
13 Letter to Jane Mander's niece Riro, undated [NZMS 535 APL].
14 Jane Mander, 'My Life in Two Worlds', *Daily Chronicle*, 28 October 1928 [NZMS 535 APL].

Chapter Eleven

1   Vernon Knowles, 'Four Writers – A Passing Scrutiny', *The Register*, Adelaide, 15 December 1928 [NZMS 535 APL].
2   Monte Holcroft, *The Way of a Writer* (Whatamongo Bay, New Zealand: Cape Catley Ltd, 1984), p. 118.
3   *Ibid.*, p. 119.
4   Jane Mander, 'Round the Town – A London Letter', *Sun* (Christ-church) 3 June 1925 [NZMS 535 APL].
5   Letter to Johannes Andersen, 18 November 1935 [Ms Papers 1186-16 ATL].
6   Monroe Wheeler later became the director of exhibitions and publications at the Museum of Modern Art, New York, 1941-1967 (Museum of Modern Art web site).
7   Notes to Dorothea Turner from Una Platts, 8 August 1964.
8   Letter to Monte Holcroft, 9 November 1931 [ATL].
9   *Ibid.*

[10] Letter to Monte Holcroft, 9 May 1932 [ATL].

[11] Letter to Monte Holcroft, from *Rangitiki* 'In the Pacific' [ATL].

[12] *Ibid.*

Chapter Twelve

[1] Letter from Maud Graham to Dorothea Turner, 11 May 1965. Private collection.

[2] 'Growing Market for NZ Novels, Ten Minutes with Jane Mander', *The Bookman, New Zealand Observer*, 10 November 1932, p. 6 [NZMS 535 APL].

[3] 'Modern Authorship, Conditions Abroad, Jane Mander Arrives', *Auckland Star*, 27 October 1932 [NZMS 535 APL].

[4] Letter to Monte Holcroft, 23 December 1932 [ATL].

[5] Notes from Una Platt to Dorothea Turner, 1964. Private collection.

[6] 'Some Random Recollections from the 1930s' by Warwick Lawrence, 1995.

[7] Letter to Monte Holcroft, 24 March 1933 [ATL].

[8] *Ibid.*

[9] *Ibid.*

[10] Letter to Monte Holcroft, 12 June 1933 [ATL].

[11] Letter to Monte Holcroft, 2 November 1933 [ATL].

[12] Monte Holcroft, *The Way of a Writer,* pp. 165, 166.

[13] Ibid., p. 167.

[14] Letter to Monte Holcroft, 25 September 1933 [ATL].

[15] Jane Mander, 'New Zealand Novelists – An Analysis and Some Advice', *The Press*, 10 November 1934 [NZMS 535 APL].

[16] Ngaio Marsh, 'The Novelist's Problem', specially written for *The Press*, 22 December 1934 [NZMS 535 APL].

Chapter Thirteen

[1] Letter to Monte Holcroft, 17 May 1934 [ATL].

[2] Letter to Monte Holcroft, 7 June 1934 [ATL].

[3] Letter to Monte Holcroft, 15 June 1938 [ATL].

[4] Letter to Monte Holcroft, 11 October 1934 [ATL].

[5] Letter to Frank Sargeson, 29 June 1936(?) [ATL].

[6] Michael King, *Frank Sargeson: A Life* (Auckland: Penguin Books (NZ) Ltd, 1995), p. 167.

[7] Letter to Frank Sargeson, dated 'Sunday', but probably 1938 from internal evidence [Sargeson Collection ATL].

[8] Letter to Johannes Andersen, 1 March 1935 [ATL].

[9] Johannes C. Andersen, *New Zealand Authors' Week 1936* (Wellington: NZ Authors' Week Committee, 1936), p. 101.

[10] Letter to Johannes Andersen, 1 March 1935 [ATL].

[11] Letter to Monte Holcroft, 10 August 1935 [ATL].

[12] Letter to Monte Holcroft, 22 February 1936 [ATL].

[13] Letter to Monte Holcroft, 22 February 1936 [ATL].

[14] This talk can be read in its original manuscript at the Auckland Central City Library [NZMS 535 Box 2 File 18].

Chapter Fourteen

1. Jane Mander, 'New Zealand Novels: The Struggle Against Environment', *The Press*, 15 December 1934.
2. Terry Sturm (ed.), *The Oxford History of New Zealand Literature* (Auckland: Oxford University Press, 1991), p. 575.
3. Letter to John A. Lee, 30 September (?1935) [APL NZMS 441/15].
4. Letter to John A. Lee, 1 March (?1936) [APL NZMS 441/15].
5. Supplement to the *New Zealand Gazette*, 27 May 1937.
6. Frank Sargeson, 'North Auckland Story', *Auckland Star*, 25 June 1938: [NZMS 535 APL].
7. Letter to John Schroder, 7 June 1938 [ATL].
8. Letter to Monte Holcroft, 15 June 1938 [ATL].
9. Monte Holcroft, 'Twenty Years After, Reissue of a Fine New Zealand Novel', *The Press*, June 1938 [NZMS 535 APL].
10. Jane Mander, 'Preface to Reminiscences' [NZMS 535 APL].
11. *Ibid.*
12. Letter to Monte Holcroft, 17 September 1942 [ATL]
13. *Ibid.*
14. *Ibid.*
15. Letter to Monte Holcroft, 13 May 1945 [ATL]
16. *Ibid.*

Chapter Fifteen

1. Personal conversation with Judy Beetham, 1996.
2. Jane Mander, *The Story of a New Zealand River*, p. 8.
3. *Ibid.*, p. 50.
4. *Ibid.*, p. 45.
5. *Ibid.*, p. 51.
6. *Ibid.*, p. 169.
7. *Ibid.*, p. 289.
8. Joan Stevens, 'Pathfinders in Fiction,' *N.Z. Listener*, 5 May 1961, p. 12 [University of Auckland Library].
9. Personal conversation with Rangi Cross, 1995.
10. 'Variations on a Theme', *20/20*, TV3, Auckland, 18 July 1994.
11. Conversation with Bob Harvey, January 1997.
12. 'Variations on a Theme', *20/20*.
13. Jane Mander, *The Story of a New Zealand River*, p. 36.
14. Vernon Knowles, 'Four Writers – A Passing Scrutiny', *The Register*, Adelaide, 15 December 1928 [NZMS 535 APL].
15. Letter to Monte Holcroft, 17 May 1934 [ATL].

BIBLIOGRAPHY

≈

Novels by Jane Mander

The Story of a New Zealand River, New York: John Lane, 1920; London: The
Bodley Head, 1920

The Passionate Puritan, London: John Lane, The Bodley Head, 1921; New York:
John Lane & co., 1922.

The Strange Attraction, New York: Dodd Mead & Co., 1922, and London: John
Lane, The Bodley Head, 1923

Allen Adair, London: Hutchinson, 1925

The Besieging City: A Novel of New York, London: Hutchinson, 1926

Pins and Pinnacles, London: Hutchinson, 1928

Primary Sources

SHORT STORIES, NEWSPAPER AND MAGAZINE ARTICLES BY JANE MANDER
These are held in the Auckland Central City Library, NZMS 535.

LETTERS FROM JANE MANDER
To Mrs Cross, her sister Tommy, are held in the Auckland Central City Library,
NZMS 535.

To Johannes C. Andersen, Eileen Duggan, Monte Holcroft, John Schroder, Mr
Moore and Mrs Wilson are held in the Alexander Turnbull Library,
Wellington.

To Mr Hacket, John A. Lee, and *The Triad* are held in the Auckland Central City
Library, NZMS 535.

To Pat Lawlor are held at the University of Auckland Library.

OTHER
Turner, Dorothea, *Jane Mander*, New York: Twayne Publishers Inc., 1972

Secondary Sources

Andersen, Johannes C., *New Zealand Authors' Week*, Wellington: NZ Authors'
Week Committee, 1936.

Brett, Sir Henry and Henry Hook, *The Albertlanders: Brave Pioneers of the '60s*,
Auckland: The Brett Printing Co. Ltd, 1927, reprint Capper Press, 1978.

Callahan, Lisa, 'Sing Sing Prison', in *Encyclopaedia of American Prisons*, edited by
Marilyn D. McShane and Frank P. Williams III, New York: Garland
Publishing Inc., 1996.

Centennial of Albertland 1862-1962, Wellsford: Campbell Press.

Chamberlain, Rudolph W., *There is no Truce: A Life of Thomas Mott Osborne*,
Freeport, New York: 1935.

Coon, Horace, *Columbia Collossus on the Hudson*, New York: E.P. Dutton & Company Inc, 1947.

Diamond, John T. and Bruce W. Hayward, *Waitakere Kauri: A Pictorial History of the Kauri Timber Industry in the Waitakere Ranges West Auckland*, Auckland: Lodestar Press, 1980.

Evatt, The Hon Mr Justice, Herbert Vere, *Australian Labour Leader: The Story of W.A. Holman and the Labour Movement*, Sydney: Angus and Robertson Ltd, 1940.

Gillespie, Oliver, 'Jane Mander: A Radio Portrait', New Zealand Public Radio, 1955.

Gurr, Andrew, *Writers in Exile: The Identity of Home in Modern Literature*, Brighton, Sussex: 1982.

Haigh, Bill, *Foote Prints Among the Kauri*, Whangarei: Bill Haigh.

Holcroft, Monte, *The Way of a Writer*, Whatamongo Bay: Cape Catley Ltd, 1984.

King, Michael, *Frank Sargeson: A Life*, Auckland: Penguin Books (NZ) Ltd, 1995.

Lawlor, Pat, *Confessions of a Journalist*, Wellington: Whitcombe & Tombs Ltd, 1936.

Lewis, Margaret, *Ngaio Marsh: A Life*, Wellington: Bridget Williams Books Ltd, 1991.

Linnell, R.T.V., *Centennial of Kaiwaka: Rautau o Kaiwaka 1859-1959*, Commemorative Booklet & Souvenir Programme, Wellsford: Campbell Press, 1959.

McFarlane, D., *Military Pensions in Auckland: A Reappraisal of the Royal New Zealand Fencibles*, MA Thesis, University of Auckland, 1981.

New York Times, 31 August 1915.

Paul, Mary, *Reading Readings: Some Current Crtitical Debates About New Zealand Literature and Culture*, PhD Thesis, University of Auckland, 1995.

Peck, Mary Gray, *Carrie Chapman Catt: A Biography*, New York: H. W. Wilson Company, 1944.

Reed, A.H., *The Kauri*, Wellington: A.H. & A.W. Reed, 1967.

— *The Gumdiggers*, Wellington: A.H. & A.W. Reed, 1972.

Sturm, Terry (editor), *The Oxford History of New Zealand Literature*, Auckland: Oxford University Press, 1991.

Watson, A.P. *Hill of the Sea Bird: In the times of the Kaipara Coates Families*, Whangarei: Allied Graphics Ltd, 1993.

Zimmerman, Elaine (compiler), *Wellsford and District Schools Centennial Booklet 1875-1975*.

INDEX

More New Zealand Literature from Otago

NOR THE YEARS CONDEMN
ROBIN HYDE

A classic New Zealand novel, in which Hyde shows the predicament of returned servicemen and women after the First World War. Through the story of Douglas Stark, we see the many ways in which New Zealand was failing their expectations. It was not the 'land fit for heroes' they had fought for, but a changing society moving through the tough times of the twenties and thirties.

292 pages, ISBN 0 908659 83 1, $29.95

WEDNESDAY'S CHILDREN
ROBIN HYDE

A fantasy about male/female relations, first published in 1937. Set affectionately in 1930s Auckland, this novel creates a heroine set on self determination and a huge joke against the reader.

'It was Shakespeare who in after years kept saying to me, "To thine own self be true". And then when it all went so badly – living where I wasn't wanted, and looking such an insignificant plain kichen pot, and dropping stitches in knitted bedsocks no sane person would have worn, anyway, I began to wonder "Which self? True to which self?"'

224 pages, ISBN 908569 72 6, $24.95

CURVED HORIZON
AN AUTOBIOGRAPHY
RUTH DALLAS

At a time when Fairburn, Glover and others spoke bitterly of the lack of support given to New Zealand artists, how did a single woman from Southland live and work as a writer, establishing herself as a poet and author of international regard?

In *Curved Horizon* Ruth Dallas writes about growing up in the 1930s, writing poetry for the children's pages of newspapers, her first publications (including the classic children's novel *The Children in the Bush*), and her involvement in the literary journal *Landfall*.

192 pages, photographs, ISBN 0 908659 54 8, $19.95

If you enjoy reading biographies, try these books from Otago

SHE DARED TO SPEAK
CONNIE BIRCHFIELD'S STORY

The story of a spirited and courageous woman who was driven by a concern for the welfare of ordinary people. Written by her daughter Maureen Birchfield, it has a liveliness and immediacy which would be difficult for an outsider to achieve.

Connie Birchfield grew up in Lancashire – working in a cotton mill from the age of thirteen – and emigrated to New Zealand in the 1920s. She became involved in unions and the Labour Party as a hotel worker, and joined the Communist Party as an unemployed worker in the 1930s. In many ways she was a woman ahead of her time – a fine street orator, a candidate in several municipal and general elections, an activist in the working women's movement – much of this while bringing up a family with a husband away at war. Her local community benefited from her organising ability and she always spoke her mind – so much so that she was expelled from the Communist Party in 1957.

This well researched and fascinating biography often reads like a novel. It is Connie Birchfield's story, pure and simple.

216 pages, photographs, ISBN 1 877133 53 1, $29.95

FOUR GENERATIONS FROM MAORIDOM
THE MEMOIRS OF A SOUTH ISLAND KAUMATUA AND FISHERMAN
BY SYD CORMACK AS TOLD TO JOANNA ORWIN

Fishing tales abound in this book, as Syd Cormack was a commercial fisherman in Moeraki and Kaikoura for much of his adult life. Even when he moved to Southland to farm, he continued fishing.

But there was another side. He describes himself as being 'four generations from Maoridom' because he was descended from an influential Moeraki woman and a European whaler. Yet his father spoke Maori and from him Syd caught the habit of collecting stories of his people, simply because he was interested. Eventually he became a recognised authority and respected kaumatua (elder), widely and frequently consulted on issues of land and genealogy.

228 pages, photographs, ISBN 1 877133 34 5, $29.95

These books are available from booksellers, libraries or from the publisher: University of Otago Press, PO Box 56, Dunedin, New Zealand. Fax (64) 09 479 8385